Parasceve paschae: or A Christians preparation to the worthy receiuing of the blessed sacrament of the Lords Supper. Newly enlarged by the R. Reuerend author, the L.B. of Land (1624)

Theophilus Field

Parasceve paschae: or A Christians preparation to the worthy receiuing of the blessed sacrament of the Lords Supper. Newly enlarged by the R. Reuerend author, the L.B. of Land
Christians preparation to the worthy receiving of the blessed sacrament of the Lords Supper
Field, Theophilus, 1574-1636.
Dedication signed: Theophilus Landavensis, i.e. Theophilus Field.
An enlargement of the edition published in 1622 as: A Christians preparation to the worthy receiuing of the blessed sacrament of the Lords Supper.
Running title reads: A preparation to the Sacrament.
[8], 224, 241-303, [1] p.
London : Printed by George Eld, for Thomas Thorp, 1624.
STC (2nd ed.) / 10861
English
Reproduction of the original in the Henry E. Huntington Library and Art Gallery

Early English Books Online (EEBO) Editions

Imagine holding history in your hands.

Now you can. Digitally preserved and previously accessible only through libraries as Early English Books Online, this rare material is now available in single print editions. Thousands of books written between 1475 and 1700 and ranging from religion to astronomy, medicine to music, can be delivered to your doorstep in individual volumes of high-quality historical reproductions.

We have been compiling these historic treasures for more than 70 years. Long before such a thing as "digital" even existed, ProQuest founder Eugene Power began the noble task of preserving the British Museum's collection on microfilm. He then sought out other rare and endangered titles, providing unparalleled access to these works and collaborating with the world's top academic institutions to make them widely available for the first time. This project furthers that original vision.

These texts have now made the full journey -- from their original printing-press versions available only in rare-book rooms to online library access to new single volumes made possible by the partnership between artifact preservation and modern printing technology. A portion of the proceeds from every book sold supports the libraries and institutions that made this collection possible, and that still work to preserve these invaluable treasures passed down through time.

This is history, traveling through time since the dawn of printing to your own personal library.

Initial Proquest EEBO Print Editions collections include:

Early Literature

This comprehensive collection begins with the famous Elizabethan Era that saw such literary giants as Chaucer, Shakespeare and Marlowe, as well as the introduction of the sonnet. Traveling through Jacobean and Restoration literature, the highlight of this series is the Pollard and Redgrave 1475-1640 selection of the rarest works from the English Renaissance.

Early Documents of World History

This collection combines early English perspectives on world history with documentation of Parliament records, royal decrees and military documents that reveal the delicate balance of Church and State in early English government. For social historians, almanacs and calendars offer insight into daily life of common citizens. This exhaustively complete series presents a thorough picture of history through the English Civil War.

Historical Almanacs

Historically, almanacs served a variety of purposes from the more practical, such as planting and harvesting crops and plotting nautical routes, to predicting the future through the movements of the stars. This collection provides a wide range of consecutive years of "almanacks" and calendars that depict a vast array of everyday life as it was several hundred years ago.

Early History of Astronomy & Space

Humankind has studied the skies for centuries, seeking to find our place in the universe. Some of the most important discoveries in the field of astronomy were made in these texts recorded by ancient stargazers, but almost as impactful were the perspectives of those who considered their discoveries to be heresy. Any independent astronomer will find this an invaluable collection of titles arguing the truth of the cosmic system.

Early History of Industry & Science

Acting as a kind of historical Wall Street, this collection of industry manuals and records explores the thriving industries of construction; textile, especially wool and linen; salt; livestock; and many more.

Early English Wit, Poetry & Satire

The power of literary device was never more in its prime than during this period of history, where a wide array of political and religious satire mocked the status quo and poetry called humankind to transcend the rigors of daily life through love, God or principle. This series comments on historical patterns of the human condition that are still visible today.

Early English Drama & Theatre

This collection needs no introduction, combining the works of some of the greatest canonical writers of all time, including many plays composed for royalty such as Queen Elizabeth I and King Edward VI. In addition, this series includes history and criticism of drama, as well as examinations of technique.

Early History of Travel & Geography

Offering a fascinating view into the perception of the world during the sixteenth and seventeenth centuries, this collection includes accounts of Columbus's discovery of the Americas and encompasses most of the Age of Discovery, during which Europeans and their descendants intensively explored and mapped the world. This series is a wealth of information from some the most groundbreaking explorers.

Early Fables & Fairy Tales

This series includes many translations, some illustrated, of some of the most well-known mythologies of today, including Aesop's Fables and English fairy tales, as well as many Greek, Latin and even Oriental parables and criticism and interpretation on the subject.

Early Documents of Language & Linguistics

The evolution of English and foreign languages is documented in these original texts studying and recording early philology from the study of a variety of languages including Greek, Latin and Chinese, as well as multilingual volumes, to current slang and obscure words. Translations from Latin, Hebrew and Aramaic, grammar treatises and even dictionaries and guides to translation make this collection rich in cultures from around the world.

Early History of the Law

With extensive collections of land tenure and business law "forms" in Great Britain, this is a comprehensive resource for all kinds of early English legal precedents from feudal to constitutional law, Jewish and Jesuit law, laws about public finance to food supply and forestry, and even "immoral conditions." An abundance of law dictionaries, philosophy and history and criticism completes this series.

Early History of Kings, Queens and Royalty

This collection includes debates on the divine right of kings, royal statutes and proclamations, and political ballads and songs as related to a number of English kings and queens, with notable concentrations on foreign rulers King Louis IX and King Louis XIV of France, and King Philip II of Spain. Writings on ancient rulers and royal tradition focus on Scottish and Roman kings, Cleopatra and the Biblical kings Nebuchadnezzar and Solomon.

Early History of Love, Marriage & Sex

Human relationships intrigued and baffled thinkers and writers well before the postmodern age of psychology and self-help. Now readers can access the insights and intricacies of Anglo-Saxon interactions in sex and love, marriage and politics, and the truth that lies somewhere in between action and thought.

Early History of Medicine, Health & Disease

This series includes fascinating studies on the human brain from as early as the 16th century, as well as early studies on the physiological effects of tobacco use. Anatomy texts, medical treatises and wound treatment are also discussed, revealing the exponential development of medical theory and practice over more than two hundred years.

Early History of Logic, Science and Math

The "hard sciences" developed exponentially during the 16th and 17th centuries, both relying upon centuries of tradition and adding to the foundation of modern application, as is evidenced by this extensive collection. This is a rich collection of practical mathematics as applied to business, carpentry and geography as well as explorations of mathematical instruments and arithmetic; logic and logicians such as Aristotle and Socrates; and a number of scientific disciplines from natural history to physics.

Early History of Military, War and Weaponry

Any professional or amateur student of war will thrill at the untold riches in this collection of war theory and practice in the early Western World. The Age of Discovery and Enlightenment was also a time of great political and religious unrest, revealed in accounts of conflicts such as the Wars of the Roses.

Early History of Food

This collection combines the commercial aspects of food handling, preservation and supply to the more specific aspects of canning and preserving, meat carving, brewing beer and even candy-making with fruits and flowers, with a large resource of cookery and recipe books. Not to be forgotten is a "the great eater of Kent," a study in food habits.

Early History of Religion

From the beginning of recorded history we have looked to the heavens for inspiration and guidance. In these early religious documents, sermons, and pamphlets, we see the spiritual impact on the lives of both royalty and the commoner. We also get insights into a clergy that was growing ever more powerful as a political force. This is one of the world's largest collections of religious works of this type, revealing much about our interpretation of the modern church and spirituality.

Early Social Customs

Social customs, human interaction and leisure are the driving force of any culture. These unique and quirky works give us a glimpse of interesting aspects of day-to-day life as it existed in an earlier time. With books on games, sports, traditions, festivals, and hobbies it is one of the most fascinating collections in the series.

The BiblioLife Network

This project was made possible in part by the BiblioLife Network (BLN), a project aimed at addressing some of the huge challenges facing book preservationists around the world. The BLN includes libraries, library networks, archives, subject matter experts, online communities and library service providers. We believe every book ever published should be available as a high-quality print reproduction; printed on-demand anywhere in the world. This insures the ongoing accessibility of the content and helps generate sustainable revenue for the libraries and organizations that work to preserve these important materials.

The following book is in the "public domain" and represents an authentic reproduction of the text as printed by the original publisher. While we have attempted to accurately maintain the integrity of the original work, there are sometimes problems with the original work or the micro-film from which the books were digitized. This can result in minor errors in reproduction. Possible imperfections include missing and blurred pages, poor pictures, markings and other reproduction issues beyond our control. Because this work is culturally important, we have made it available as part of our commitment to protecting, preserving, and promoting the world's literature.

GUIDE TO FOLD-OUTS MAPS and OVERSIZED IMAGES

The book you are reading was digitized from microfilm captured over the past thirty to forty years. Years after the creation of the original microfilm, the book was converted to digital files and made available in an online database.

In an online database, page images do not need to conform to the size restrictions found in a printed book. When converting these images back into a printed bound book, the page sizes are standardized in ways that maintain the detail of the original. For large images, such as fold-out maps, the original page image is split into two or more pages

Guidelines used to determine how to split the page image follows:

- Some images are split vertically; large images require vertical and horizontal splits.
- For horizontal splits, the content is split left to right.
- For vertical splits, the content is split from top to bottom.
- For both vertical and horizontal splits, the image is processed from top left to bottom right.

Parasceve Paschæ:

OR A CHRISTIANS PREPARATION TO THE WORTHY
receiuing of the blessed Sacrament of the Lords Supper.

Newly enlarged by the R. Reuerend Author, *the* L. B. *of* Land.

LONDON,
Printed by *George Eld*, for *Thomas Thorp.* 1 6 2 4.

TO THE HIGH AND MIGHTY PRINCE GEORGE DVKE OF Buckingham, &c.

High and Illustrious Prince:

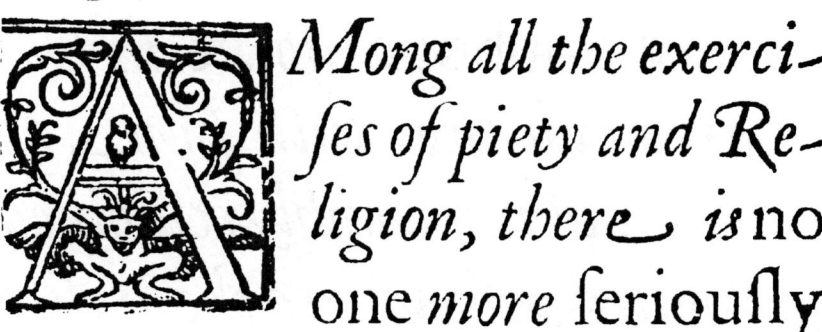Mong all the *exercises of piety and Religion, there* is no one *more seriously to be intended, and (if so done)* none more *aduantagious to a Christian soule, then the worthy*

A2   recei-

The Epistle

receiuing of the blessed Sacrament of the Body and Blood of our Lord and Sauiour Iesus Christ: whereby we are incorporated into Christ, and made true & liuely members of him: nay, whereby as hee, by his Incarnation was made flesh of our flesh, and bone of our bone: so we in spirit are made one with him, so neerly and inseparably conioined & vnited, as (maugre the malice of the deuill) we cannot be seuered from him; but whither hee, our head, is gone before vs, wee, his

his members, *shall follow after him. To whō should I make choice to present these assured meanes of attaining that eternall happiness, rather then to your* Grace, *a true louer of Piety and true Religion: to who as I owe my* best *of temporall things (next to* God *and the* King*) so (according to the inuersion of Saint* Pauls rule*) I ought to pay the* best *of things* spirituall.

This little Treatise therefore (a helpe to that heauenly treasure) I humbly dedicate to your Grace;

Grace; *as being not onely the first* Author *of my* wel-being, *but (if so* meane *deserts may haue any future* hopes) *the* Finisher *of my* better-being.

It was formerly (by a preuailing Friend) *extorted from me, and* exposed *to the open world; when it was,* then, *but an* imperfect *and* vn-shapen Embryon: But now (*sithens it hath gotten its* perfect limbs, *and* trueshape *and feature, & hath learned to* speake plainly, *without any* lisping *affectation) it hath*

a

Dedicatory.

a great desire to be preferred to your Honors seruice: where if it do prosper & come forward, the Father and Friends of it shal become hūble suters to Almighty God, that as he (by the hands of our Soueraigne) hath formerly *heaped on your* Noble person, Honour *vpon* Honour; *so he will be pleased* still to adde grace *vnto your* Grace *here in* this *world, and in the* next crown you with glory after glory.

Your *Graces* most bounden in
all duty and seruice,
Theophilus Landavensis.

Parasceve Paschæ:
OR,
A CHRISTIANS PREPARATION TO
the worthy recciuing of the
blessed Sacrament of the
Lords Supper.

VR blessed Sauiour making mention of *his Bodie and Bloud*, calleth it *the Bread of Life*, And in the 51 verse of the same Chapter, hee further saith, *The Bread, that I will giue, is my flesh; which I will giue for the life of the world.* Yet this Bread and this Flesh is not *Life* to *All.* For to some it is *Death*

Iohn 6.48.

B   and

and *Destruction*. For, *Hee that eateth and drinketh vnworthily, eateth and drinketh his owne damnation.*

1.Cor.11.29.

'Tis very strange, that *so Contrary* effects, (as Life & Death) should spring out of *one* and the *selfe-same Cause.* Doth a Fountaine *send out at one place bitter water and sweet*, saith S. *Iames*? That may not be granted. And yet the same *Sacrament* of Christ his blessed Bodie and Blood, *Mors est malis, vita Bonis,* as *Aquinas* speaketh; It is *Death to the wicked and vnworthy, and Life to the godly and worthy Receiuer.* But, Certainly, these two *Contrary* effects doe not *Naturally* proceed from the Sacrament *it selfe*: but the *One*, (*viz.* Death) is caused by *It*, no otherwise then *accidentally*, and *improperly*. For the Sacra-

Iames 3.11.

In Hymno.

Sacrament it selfe was ordained by Christ, to bee an *Instrument of spirituall Life*; and no cause of *Death* or *Damnation* at all. But wee haue a *common* saying in the Schooles, That *Omnis causa agit secundum dispositionem Subiecti*; Euery cause doth worke according as the *Subiect*, (which it is to worke vpon) is fitted and disposed. Therefore *Experience* sheweth, that *one* and the *same Heate* of the *same* Sunne, doth *Harden* the Clay, and *melt*, or *mollifie* the Wax. The *same meat*, doth nourish and strengthen an *healthful & sound* body; which, if it be eaten by persons of *sicke* and *corrupted* stomacks, doth but increase their Disease, and degenerate into the malignant humour of the *sicknesse* it selfe. So, howsoeuer the Sacrament of the Lords body doth *augment grace* in the *prepared heart* of a *penitent Receiuer*: yet the *impenitent* and *obstinate* sinner, by partaking of that holy mysterie, becomes more sicke in Soule, and more crazed in conscience, then before. *That* happeneth to him *in Soule*, which is reported to haue befaln *Henry* the *Emperour in his body*; *Cui in hostiâ consecratâ venenum attulit interitum*, Who was poisoned by receiuing the consecrated Host. The Arke of the Couenant receiued into the house of *Obed-Edom* (for the space of 3 moneths) brought great benefits, and much happinesse with it. *For the Lord blessed* Obed-Edom, *and all his houshold*. Yet for all that, the *Philistims* had the same Arke amongst them, for a much longer

Sabellicus lib. 8.

2. Sam. 6. 10.

ger time; and they were so far from reaping any benefit or benediction by it, that the Lord powred his curses and plagues vpon them, *for deteining it.* The reason of which different effects, was the *Difference* and *Dissimilituae* of the *Lodging* or *Roome* into which the Arke was receiued. *Obed-Edom* entertained it with all humble reuerence, and pious deuotion of a sanctified heart: The Philistims receiued it so *indeuoutly* and *vnreuerently*, that they forbare not to place it by their *Idol Dagon*. So this heauenly Sacrament becommeth *Death to the bad, and Life to the good* : by reason of the diuerse disposition, and different preparation of those persons which are partakers of it. *Some* (like *Obed-Edom*) prepare their Soules be-

1.Sam. 5.2.

B 3 fore-

fore-hand, to receiue it with *Faith, Penitence, Humilitie*, and *Reuerence*. Others (like the *Philistims*) make no such reckoning of it, but receiue it *hand ouer head*, into an impenitent, an vnsanctified, and an vnprepared heart; an heart *wedded* to wickednesse, and do place it among their *deare* and *darling* sinnes; which they *doat* vpon, and *adore* no lesse, then if they were their *Idols*. That therefore wee may know *how* to receiue this food of our soules in such manner; as it may bring *Life*, and *Grace*, and *Saluation* to vs, the *Apostle* setteth vs downe the way, in his first *Epistle* to the *Corinths*, the 11 *Chapter* at the 28 *verse*. *Let a man therefore examine himselfe, &c.*

Which words of the blessed Apostle containe a *double charge*:

to the Sacrament.

charge: First, that *we try* before we *eate*; and secondly, that *we eate* after tryall.

Before we do communicate, the Apostle requires *triall of our selues*: and then, *after triall and Examination*, hee commands vs to communicate. And so he encounters with *two sorts of men*; whereof the *One* eates of this Bread, and *Tries not*: and those offend against the *first part*. The other try themselues; but *doe not eat* of *this Bread*: and these faile against *the second*.

The *first* enioyneth a *preparation*; in these words: [*Let a man therefore examine himselfe.*]

The *second* commandeth a *participation*; in these words: [*And so let him eat of this bread and drinke of this Cup.*]

A Preparation

In the *preparation*, we may, for our *purpose*, consider these *three things*.

First, a *duty* enioyned; which is, to *Try*, *Proue*, or *Examine*.

Secondly, the *person commanded* to performe this Dutie; which is, *Euery man*; in this word, Ἄνθρωπος.

Thirdly, the *party* to be *examined*; in this word ἑαυτὸν *himselfe*.

Concerning the *Dutie*, wee are to insist vpon foure things.

First, the *action* it selfe, which is a *Tryall*.

Secondly, the *necessity* of this Action; in this *Illatiue* : *Therefore*.

Thirdly, the *manner* of it, out of the *Nature* of the word, δοκιμάζειν.

Fourthly, the *subiect matter*, or the *things whereof* wee are

to

to examine our selues.

But, because that the *Duty* is an *Action*, which doth presuppose an *Agent*; and because that *every Agent* is moued and stirred vp to worke by the *Obiect*: Therefore wee will *first* treat of the *Agent*, which is the *party* here charged to examine.

Secondly, of the *party to bee examined*.

Lastly, of the *Action*, or duty of *examination* it selfe.

1. The *Agent*, or *person* here charged with this *Duty* of *Examinatiō*, is expressed vnder this word ἄνθρωπος, or *Homo*; which doth include not onely *both sexes*, but also *all degrees*. For ἄνθρωπος, in Greeke; and *Homo* in Latine, are both *Masculine* and *Fœminine*, containing both male and female, both man and woman.

woman. So, that, *by this*, euery *woman* that is *capable* of this *Sacrament* is bound to try and examine *her selfe*, no lesse then *Men* are.

Neither doe they include *both* the *Sexes* onely; but also *all degrees* of persons: Prince and people; learned and ignorant; Rich and Poore; Laymen, and Church-men. For ἄνθρωπος, and *Homo*, are the *Genus* to all that doe weare the *Nature* of *Man* about them. So that euery *Lay-person* is lyable to this charge as well as the *Minister* of God; the *Nobles* and *Princes* of the world are bound to the performance of this Duty no lesse then the *meanest* among the people.

—— *Rex Iupiter omnibus Idem.*
God is the *same God to all*; and requireth equall *obedience* from All. *Regum*

Regum timendorum in proprios Greges,
Reges in ipsos Imperium est Iouis.

All that are *capable* of the Sacrament of Christs body and blood are brought within the *compasse* of this *Charge.* And therefore they, who *willingly*, and *wilfully* do neglect the dutie of examining themselues, are guilty of *grieuous sinne*, 1. *Cor.* 11. 27. I say *all that are capable.* For indeed *some* there be which are *not capable* of this Sacrament, nor *able* to conceiue either of their *owne miserie* by sin, nor of the *deepe mysteries* contained in the Supper of the Lord: and *such* are discharged, *as* from the participation of the Sacrament, *so* from this duty of examining themselues.

Of this *Number* are *Infants,* yong *Children,* Ideots, *Madmen,* and *others* that are *accidentally*

dentally *depriued* of the *right vse* of Reason and Vnderstanding.

Saint *Cyprian* (*de lapsis, Serm.* 5.) tels vs of a *Deacon* that would needs force a young Girle to receiue the *Cup of the Lord*, and powred the *consecrated Wine* into her mouth: though the *child* was not able to keepe it in her stomacke, but *deliuered* it backe againe.

And S. *Augustine* (*de Eccl: Dogmat. lib.* 1. *cap.* 51.) and S. *Ierome* (*contra Luciferian*:) report that *all* that were *baptized*, (as well *children* as *others*,) immediately receiued the Holy Sacrament of the Eucharist. For *some* in the *Primitiue Church* held it not onely *conuenient*, but *necessary*, that the holy Communion should bee administred to *all* that had receiued

ued *Baptisme* (euen to *Infants*) that, *by it*, the remission and pardon of their sinnes might be sealed to their soules.

But this *Tenet* was in them a *great*, but yet a *pious Errour*. For considering that Babes and Infants, for *want* of the vse of *Reason* and *Iudgement*, can neither *declare* the Lords Death, nor *discerne the Lords body*, nor take a *due examination* of their owne consciences, by sitting *in Iudgement* vpon themselues, as they ought, 1. *Cor.* 11. 31. It is not possible that they should become *meet* and *worthy* receiuers of the Lords body. Therefore in the *Old Testament* wee see, that *Circumcision* (which was to *them*, the Sacrament *of Regeneration*, and *Initiation*; as *Baptisme is to vs*) was administred to Infants the 8 day after they

they were borne: But to the *eating of the Paschal Lambe* (whereunto *our Communion* answereth) *none* were admitted til they were able to *enquire and examine, Quæ est ista Religio?* What seruice, or *Religion is this which yee keepe*, Exodus 12.26.

The *like* is the *case* of all Madmen, Lunatikes, and naturall Fooles.

The charge then, of examination, must bee vnderstood *Secundum Subiectum*: Thus: Let *euery one*, that, by his good endeuours, may be *fit* and *capable* to eate this Bread and drink this Cup, take a due examination of himself. But *such* as by an *inuincible necessity* are disabled, for the present, from *discerning* the Lords Body, and so, *consequently*, from eating this Bread and

and drinking this Cup worthily, are therefore *vnable to performe* this duty of examination; and so *discharged* from it. So much for the party charged to examine.

Now followeth the *party that is to be examined*: That is, *himselfe*. [*Let euery man therefore examine himselfe:*] not *another* mans person, but *his owne* person. But the number of *those* is great, which doe here stumble at the very *threshold*. For in stead of *examining* and *confessing* their *owne sinnes* and imperfections before GOD, they take vpon them to *sift* and *censure* the faults and imperfections of *their neighbours*. Like the *vaine-glorious* and *censorious Pharisee*, who iustified himselfe, and accused *other men* to be *extortioners*, vniust, adulterers,

terers, & (*pointing at* his neighbour in *disgrace* and scorne,) called him, *This Publican,* Luke 18.11. *Nemo curiosus, quin sit Malevolus,* saith one: This curious *Inquisitiuenesse* into the liues and conuersations of *other men,* is an argument of some *secret malice* and *ill will* which we beare them; and therefore a *quality* very *ill-beseeming* a Communicant. And yet the world swarmeth with such ἀλλοτριοεπίσκοποι *Busy-bodies,* which are euer curiously and enuiously prying into *other mens liues and manners,* being most *negligent* and *carelesse* of mending their owne. They can spy *moats in another mans eye,* when they will not perceiue *huge beames in their owne,* Math. 7. 4. Their *owne sinnes* they cast into that *part of the wallet* which hangs
behind

behind their backs, but *their brethrens* faults they put into the *fore-part* which hangs euer in their sight. Wherin they do resemble the *Lamiæ*; who are feined, when they walkt *abroad*, to take their *eyes* out of a *Box*, and put thē into their *Heads*, to see what was done *of others* abroad; but as soone as they returned *home* to their own houses, they took their *eies* out of *their heads*, & put them vp in the *box*; seeing nothing at home. The reason hereof is, because we looke *forward* on *others* actions, *Oculo directo*, with a direct eye; whereas we marke not *our own* actions but *oculo reflexo*, by a kinde of reflecting back vpon our selues.

It is one of *Satans snares* which hee layeth to entangle the *soules* of men, when hee perswades a man to *compare* himselfe with

C others;

others; and to thinke, that if *hee bee* not worse then the *very worst*, and more notoriously wicked then the most profligate miscreant, hee is good *enough* for God, and needeth not to bee *any better*. For this cause, his manner is in matters of *this world* (as *Honor, profit, pleasure*) to make vs to compare our selues with such as are *before* vs: and not with those that are *behinde vs*. That is, to cast our eyes on such as liue in greater *Honour*, in more *abundance of worldly pleasure*, and haue a more *plentifull portion* of wealth and riches then wee: That so hee may driue vs to *impatience* and *murmuring* against *Gods prouidence*, which hath not dealt *so liberally*, and bountifully with vs. But *he* wil by no means, suffer vs to *reflect* vpon those that are *behinde* vs: that is, on such

such as are in *meaner estate*, and in *greater misery* and *affliction*, then we our selues are; lest we should rest *contented*: which *contentation* is a vertue so highly esteemed *by God*, that euen *godlinesse* it selfe, *without contentment*, is not esteemed.

1.Tim.6.6.

On the *other side*, in *spirituall* matters, which concerne the *euerlasting welfare* of body and soule, his fashion is, to teach vs to *compare* our selues with such as are *behinde* vs, and doe come *short* of vs in some vertues and graces, causing vs to *perswade* our selues that wee are *wondrous holy Saints*, because wee are not *incarnate Deuils*.

Whereas, if *we* did *well*, wee should take the *cleane contrary course*. That is, in *worldly* things, we should consider how many are *behinde* vs, in greater *penury*, in meaner *place*, and in greater *misery*, then we are (and yet notwithstanding *they* are of *much better deserts*, and as deare children of God, as *we*:) That so we may rest *contented* and *blesse* God for those *temporall commodities*, which it hath pleased him, in his mercy to bestow vpon vs.

And in *spirituall matters*, which concerne our eternal saluation, we should neuer looke to those that are *behind vs* in grace; but to such as are *before vs*, and doe excell vs in vertue. That, so, we may not onely be *more humbled* in our soules (considering how farre *many others* doe outstrip vs in *goodnesse*) but also, in an *holy æmulation*, may striue to grow from *grace to grace*, from vertue to vertue, that so at last we may *ouertake* them. Thus, a man

to the Sacrament.

man may make a *good vse* of *comparing* himselfe with other men. And *this* caused the *blessed* Apostle Saint *Paul*, forgetting that which was *behind*, to endeuour himselfe to τὰ ἔμπροσθεν, those things which were before. *Phil. 3. 13.*

The *charge* then is, that we do *reflect* vpō *our own selues*, & examine our own hearts & consciences, in what state they are; leauing *others* to be iudged of *God*, and of *their owne* Consciences.

The Church of *Rome* in their *Synode* of *Trent*, doth enioyne great *preparation* before the *Receiuing* and participation of this Sacrament. But this *preparation* (as they say) consisteth *chiefely* in an *enumeration* or *rehearsall of all* sinnes (especially of all *mortall* sinnes) which by diligent search and inquisition they can call to memorie, into *Sess. 14. ca. 5. & Sess. 7. c. 7. can. 11.*

the

the eares of a *Masse-Priest*: and *they* further maintaine that all the *godly sorrow* or *contrition* in the world will not serue the turne, to *receiue worthily*, vnlesse that, *before the Sacrament receiued*, euery person do *shriue* himselfe, and confesse *euery particular sinne* to his Confessor. And this *Auricular Confession* they hold to bee *so necessary*, *vt qui non omnia, hoc modo, confessus fuerit, illi diuinam Bonitatem, per Ministerium, seu Absolutionem, nihil remittere*: That *the goodnesse of God, by the Ministerie, or Absolution, doth not remit any sinne, except the party doe confesse all after this maner.* Thus it is concluded by the *Fathers* of that *Synode*, and *thus* it is practised by all the *Romish Catholiques* at this day.

But if *this Auricular Confession*

to the Sacrament.

sion bee an *ingredient* so necessarie to the preparation of receiuing the Lords body *worthily*, it is very strange that G O D should not leaue vs any *Commandement* touching it, neither in the *Old* nor in the *New* Testament. For *Gratian*, *Bonauenture*, *Panormitan*, *Scotus*, & *Georgius Cassander*, *Archbishop of Triers*, cannot perswade *themselues* that *it* hath any *ground* either in the *Old* or in the *New* Testament: neither are *they* resolued that the *Apostles* did leaue it to the *Church* by *Tradition*.

Moreouer, this *Auricular Confession* doth transforme the *Gospell* into the *Law*, by hanging and *fastening* the remission of sinnes, not vpon *onely faith in Christ Iesus*, but vpon the *deed* & worke of a *Man*; namely, vpon the *enumeration* and recounting of *every particular sinne*, which hee hath committed, together with *all* the *circumstances*.

Besides all this, such a scrupulous ripping vp of all and euery his sinnes, with all their circumstances, cannot but *anguish* and torment the soule with *doubts, diffidence* and *despaire*. And therfore *Archbishop Cassander* cals this Auricular confession, *Carnificinam Animarum*, a *Gibbet* of soules. For when a man sees that he cannot recollect *all* his offences; and that, *except hee doe it*, there is no *hope* of pardon and forgiuenesse; his conscience cannot but remaine *very vnquiet* and in *great perplexitie*.

And furthermore, by *enioyning* it, the Church of *Rome* commandeth *impossibilities*. For *who knoweth how often he offendeth?* saith the Psalmist.

Lastly,

Lastly, in the *Greeke Church* because it was abused to *villany* (as it hath beene in the *Romish Church* also) the *Priests* committing filthinesse with women vnder colour of Auricular confession, it was quite abolished by *Nestorius*. And therefore *Theodorus* sometimes Archbishop of *Canterbury* saith, *Græci & totus Oriens confitetur soli Deo*, The *Græcians* and all the *Easterne Church* doe confesse themselues *to God onely*.

And, *mee thinkes*, the very words, here in hand, are flat against it. For the Apostle saith, Let a man examine *himselfe*: and not, *Let another try or examine, &c.* For *none* can try or examine *thee*, so well as *thou* canst try *thy selfe*. For *thou* knowest more by *thy selfe* then *all* the world beside doth. *Thou knowest*

Distinct. 1. Quidam Deo.

knowest *certainly* whether thou dost *truly repent* and *beleeue* stedfastly in *Christ* thy Sauiour, which none but God and thine owne soule can certainly affirme.

Notwithstanding, wee are to know that the *Church of England* doth not barre the *Minister* from examining *his flocke* whether they bee furnished with *competent knowledge* concerning the *nature* and *vse* of this Sacrament: but yet *it* holdeth it not *sufficient* that a communicant haue his *Pastors approbation* and allowance; but *it* requires also, that wee *our selues* should enter into our *own hearts*, and call our *owne consciences* to examination; because *we* are *best* acquainted with our owne sufficiencies and deficiencies; with our owne wants and

to the Sacrament.

and graces. Neither doth *our Church* forbid or restraine men (if their consciences bee troubled and perplexed) to *open & confesse some particular* sinnes to the *Minister* of Christ: but, in *such cases* it exhorteth them thereunto; as you may reade in the second exhortation before the *Communion*, where the *Minister* is enioyned to say *thus: viz.*

Because it is necessary that no man should come to the holy communion but with a full trust in Gods mercy, and with a quiet conscience: therefore if there be any of you, which by the meanes aforesaid, cannot quiet his owne conscience, but requireth further comfort and counsell; Then let him come unto me, or some other learned and discreet Minister of Gods word, and open his griefe

tha

A Preparation

that he may receiue such ghostly counsell, aduice, and comfort, as his conscience may bee relieued; and that by the Ministery of Gods word hee may receiue comfort and the benefit of absolution, to the quieting of his conscience, and auoiding of all scruple and doubtfulnesse.

But leauing the *party examined*, we come to the *duty* it self, in δοκιμαζέτω, *Let him try or examine*.

Every man ought *humbly to prepare and dispose his heart*, before hee presume to *heare* or *receiue* any thing that toucheth *God*. For *God* is a *Spirit*, and *we* are *flesh*; *God* is in *heauen*, and *we* on *earth*. *Pythagoras* was wont to say, *Non loquendum de Deo, sine lumine: We ought not to speake of God without light*. *That is*, without *premeditation and*

and aduised consideration, *who it is of whom wee speake*. The Wiseman saith, *Before thou pray prepare thine heart, and bee not as a man that tempteth God.* Ecclus. 18. Likewise in *old time* it was decreed, that the *Catechumeni* Clement.Epist. 3. should be warned before-hand to *prepare* their hearts, that they might *worthily* receiue *Baptisme*. And if *preparation* bee needfull to *heare*, to *pray*, to *receiue* the sacrament of *baptisme*; certainly it is as iustly required at the receiuing of the *holy communion*. Therefore *Let a man examine himselfe*.

But the *Apostle*, in this, doth seeme to *crosse* the *common course*. For *ordinarily* we vse to *examine, taste*, and *try* the *meat* it selfe wee are to feed on, and *not* the *person* who is to eate it. Thus a man would imagine at
the

the *first*. But here is no place left for the trying and prouing of *this Meat*. For *this* is *Diuine meat*, seasoned by the *Holy Ghost*, composed of the *flesh and blood* of Christ the Sonne of God, and therefore it needeth not any *præuious* or precedent *tasting* or *triall*: but it is *requisite* that the *party* which is about to feed on it, should first proue and try *himselfe*, whether *his heart* be sincere and his conscience pure. Therefore the Apostle chargeth euery one to try himselfe.

Which *Doctrine* no doubt but *hee* learned by those *things* and *actions* which were done at Christ his *last supper*. For howbeit *Saint Paul* was *not present* at that time, when *Christ* did institute this Sacrament, yet by *particular reuelation*, hee was taught

taught what manner of things were *then* done. So he himselfe witnesseth, *Gal.* 1. 12. *He receiued it not from man, but δἰ ἀποκαλύψεως, by the Reuelation of Iesus Christ.* And concerning this *Sacrament*, he saith particularly, That *whatsoeuer he deliuered, he receiued it of the Lord.* And *this* he receiued (no doubt) *among the rest*, that a man should *examine* himselfe. Therfore wheras *our Sauiour* at his last supper did strike *all* his inuited *guests* into a kind of amazement and astonishment, when he told thē, *Verily I say vnto you that one of you shal betray me.* Some of *them* might haue said to *him* againe, *Lord*, why dost thou vexe and perplex the minds of thy louing friends whom thou hast inuited to *so heauenly a feast*, with such vnseasonable mention

1 Cor.11.23.

Mat.26.21.

tion of *treason* against thy life? Why dost thou reach vs such a *bitter morsell* before those delicious dainties which thou art about to set before vs? But it pleased the wisdome of our Sauiour *so* to deale, that *euery man* might vnderstand, that *hee* was bound to *examine* his own hart diligently and strictly as the *Apostles* of Christ did *then*: For *euery one* did make enquiry concerning *himselfe*: saying, *Is it I, Master?* which act of theirs (at the very *first* institution) is left in the Church for a *patterne* and a *precept* inuiolable: whereby we are *bound* to prepare our selues to the *worthy receiuing* of this Sacrament: and this is it which S. *Paul* teacheth when he faith, *Let a man examine himselfe, and so let him eate of this bread, &c.*

Besides,

Mat.26.22.

Besides, our Sauiours *washing* of the Disciples *feet* before his Sacramentall Supper, and his *pleasure* to haue his *body*, after death, wrapped in *cleane white linnen*, and layd in a *new* Sepulchre, wherein *neuer* man was layd, do manifestly declare how *cleane and pure* wee ought to be in soule and conscience, when we do receiue the Lords body. Hence it is that Saint *Augustine* saith, *Vnusquisq; consideret conscientiam suam, & quando se aliquo graui crimine vulneratum esse cognouerit, prius studeat eam emundare; aliàs, potiùs se debet excommunicare, & ab Altari remouere, quàm aliter accedere.* To which agreeth that of *Theophilact*, vpon these words of the Apostle, *Non alium tibi judicem tribuo, sed teipsum tibi commendo: judica igitur, & explora*

Iohn 13.

Serm. 252.

plora conscientiam tuam, & sic accede.

The *greatnesse* and *sublimity* of the diuine *Maiesty*, to whom we approach, perswadeth *hereunto*; for, we come not to the *wooden Arke*, and an *Altar of gold*, nor to *manu-facta sacramenta*, and an *earthly Tabernacle*; but wee come to the *glorious Maiesty of the eternall God*, before *whom* the blessed *Angels* stand with reuerend and humble feare; & to *Christ* the *Iudge* of the quicke and the dead, before *whom* all flesh shall stand, and at *whose presence* al Kings of the earth, all Nations and Princes shall tremble; to the *true body* and *blood* of God, wherewith the *world* was redeemed.

Now the *necessity* of this dutie is inferred in this word (*therefore*,) which hath *relation* to

Acts 10.

Heb. 12. 2

to the *verse* going before, where the *Apostle* saith, that *Whosoeuer doth eate this bread, and drinke the cup of the Lord vnworthily, shall be guilty of the body and blood of the Lord*; as if hee had *murthered* his Sauiour, and shed his blood: *not* in the same *degree*, but yet in *proportion*. For looke whatsoeuer blasphemies, irrisions, scornes, contumilies and reproaches thy *miscreant* Iewes belched forth and practised corporally against Christ, the *same* are *spiritually* repeated and iterated by the vnworthy receiuer, who doth crucifie the Sonne of God againe himselfe, and make a mocke of him. Heb. 6 6.

True it is, that the best of vs all are not *worthy so much as to gather vp the crummes vnder the Lords Table*; and when wee
D 2 haue

haue done our best to prepare our selues to *receiue*, yet we are with the *Centurion* to confesse, *Domine, non sum dignus vt intres sub tectum meum*, *Lord I am not worthy that thou shouldst enter vnder my roofe*. Therefore it would be knowne what *kind* of *worthines* is here required. For the vnderstanding whereof, we are to consider, that there is in Scripture mentioned a threefold *dignity* or *worthinesse*.

The first is, ἀξιότης φυσική, a *naturall kind of worthinesse*, which consisteth in an *equality* betwixt the honour giuen, and the person receiuing it. In this sense the *foure and twenty Elders*, casting down their crowns before the Throne of God, doe say, *Thou Lord art worthy to receiue glory, and honour, and power, because thou hast created all these*

Com. Booke.

Math. 8.

Apoc. 4. last.

these things. Here is a *naturall worthinesse* equalizing the glorie and honour propounded. But this *naturall worthinesse* is not in any of the sonnes of *Adam*; For, *by nature wee are all the children of Gods wrath*, and burthened with innumerable actuall transgressions, which make vs vtterly vnworthy of the *least* of Gods mercies and fauours. *Eph. 2.*

Gen. 32.

The second, is ἀξιότης μισθωτή, a *worthinesse of equity*, by *stipulation* or bargaine: as the *labourer is worthy of his hire*, because he agreed for *so much*, and earneth it by his sweat and paines. But *this worthiness* is not in any of vs, we can challenge no such thing, but when *we haue done all that we can, wee are ingenuously to confesse, that we are all but vnprofitable seruants.* *Math. 20. 9.*

Luke 17.

The third is, ἀξιότης ἱκανότητος, *Dignitas conuenientiæ*, a worthinesse of *fitnesse* or *conuenience*. In which regard hee that commeth to the Lords table, if he bring a *competent measure* of godly sorrow and true penitence for his sinne, and a *true faith* in the promise of saluation through the *alone merits* of Iesus Christ, may bee accepted as *fit* and *conuenient* guest to eat the flesh, and drinke the blood of Christ. Hee may be worthy, as *Hales* saith, *non dignitate suâ, sed dignatione Diuinâ*, Though *not* by any *worthinesse inherent* in himselfe, yet by Gods *gratious acceptation*, who is contented to accept such a person for a fit and worthy Communicant.

The *manner* of this examination, is, that it must be exact, strict,

strict, and sincere. For so much doth the word δοκιμάζειν import. It is a word borrowed from the *Gold-smiths*, who to try & examine their *mettals* whether they be *pure*, or *counterfeit* and false, doe bring them to the *Test* or *Touchstone*: So *wee*, before we come to the Lords table, must put our selues to the *Test*, and make an exact triall of our soules. Which, if wee doe once set out our selues to doe *seriously*, then wee, euery one of vs, shall find *our selues* to bee a *whole New-found world* of sin and wickednesse. Nay: what doe I speak of the whole man? when as one little member of man, *his Tongue*, is by the vnerring language of the Holy Ghost, styled *a world of wickednesse*. What a bottomlesse Abysse of iniquity then is to bee

Iames 3.5.

D 4   found

found in the whole man?

The fraudulency of mans heart is vnsearchable by any on earth, sauing by the *spirit* and conscience of a mans own selfe: we must therefore call *our selues* to examination before our *own consciences*, which will either *accuse vs or excuse vs in the things that we haue done*. If our *heart* condemn vs, *God is greater then our heart, & knoweth all things*: but if our *owne heart* condemne vs not, then haue wee *boldnesse* towards God. We are not then to dissemble or excuse *any manner* of sinne, be it *neuer so deare* vnto vs : lest that in *so* doing, we kindle Gods wrath against vs, and *prouoke him to plague vs*, rather then appease and mitigate his anger towards vs. One saith, that *Conscientia est scientia cum Scientiâ. Scientia in nobis cum*

Rom. 2. 15.

1 Iohn 3. 21. 22.

to the Sacrament.   41

cum aliâ Scientiâ in Deo congruens. A knowledge in *vs* agreeing with another knowledge which is in God. In which regard some haue compared the Conscience to a *Tally.* Bakers and Brewers (and such Trades-men as vse to deliuer their commodities to their Customers vpon *Tale*) are wont (*Taleolare*) to cleaue a stick in *twaine*, and to deliuer to their Customers the *one side of it*, keeping the *other side* to themselues, and euer as they deliuer out their wares, they make a certain number of *Marks* and *Nicks* vpon both parts of their Tallies, to keep euen reckonings: So that if either goe about to deceiue other, they need but to draw out *their side* of the Tally, and *that* will soone discouer the *Truth.* Euery action which proceedeth from vs (bee it *good* or *bad*) is

markt

markt and nickt vpon the Tally of Gods Science and our Conscience: if we haue laboured to *deface* or *scrape* out any thing that hath beene marked on our side of the Tally, God needs but draw out that which is *markt* on his side; and *that* will soone conuince vs of Fraud. For *God is greater then our heart*. And therfore it concernes vs very much to deale *truely* and *vprightly* with him.

From the *manner* of our examination, I proceed to the *matter* concerning which euery Communicant must bee tryed; and they may bee reduced to these two; namely, *Repentance* and ~~*Charitie.*~~ *Faith*.

Vnder *Repentance* I doe include *Charitie*. For hee that vpon the *sight* of his owne corruption and wickednesse, hath learned

learned to renounce and forsake *himselfe*, and to *resigne* vp himselfe to the obedience of Christ, doubtlesse will earnestly endeuour to practise all the duties of *Charity*, commended *so often* by Christ, and commanded in the first and second Table of the Decalogue.

We attaine to *Repentance*, by the *sight* and *knowledge* of our *sinnes*. Our *sinnes* are discouered, and *made knowne* vnto vs by the *Law* of God. Euery sin is as a *spot* or *staine* vpon the Soule; and the *Law* of God is a *Looking-glasse* of the Soule, which sheweth euery spot and wrinckle. It is behoouefull then for euery one to set *this Glasse* before him, and according *to it*, to examine the *beauty* or *deformitie* of his Soule. The summe of this *Law of God* is comprised in

Iam. 1. 21.
sacra Scriptura, quasi speculum quoddam, mentis oculis obiicitur: ibi pulchra nostra in Christo prospicimus, ibi fœda nostra in nobis cernimus. Bern. in moralib.

in the *Decalogue*, or *ten Commandements*. Which Commandements are divided into *two Tables*. The *First*, containing the duties which wee *owe vnto God*: The *second*, the duties which wee *owe vnto our neighbour*. The *first*, commandeth all maner of *Holinesse*, that wee owe to God : the *second* commandeth *Righteousnesse* to our Neighbour.

The Commandements contained in the *first Table* are foure. The first whereof is this.

I. COMMANDEMENT.
Thou shalt haue none other Gods but me.

The maine *duty* commanded in these words, is the inward honour of the heart, and the branches of it be seuen.

1 The acknowledging of
the

to the Sacrament.

the True God, as he hath *reuealed himselfe* in his Word. | Iohn 4.24.
Rom. 1.21.
Deut. 6.13.

2 To *feare* him more then all. | Esay 8.13.

3 To *loue* him aboue all creatures in heauen and earth. | Deut. 6.5.

4 To put all our *confidence* and trust in him. | Psal. 91.1,2.

5 To *humble* our selues before him. | Reu. 4.11.

6 To be *patient*, and content with what he is pleased to send, or lay vpon vs. | Mal. 3.14.

7 To *Hope* in him onely.

Sinnes forbbidden in this commandement are:

1 *Ignorance* of the true God, *false opinions* touching the *Essence*, and *will* of God, *Superstition*, *Idolatry*, *trusting* in creatures. | Sap. 1.1.
Col. 3.5.
Ephes. 5.5.
Phil. 3.8.
Luke 16.9.
1 Tim. 6.17.

2 *Carnall* securitie, and contempt of God. | Psal. 14.4.

3 *Hating* of God, or a *coun-*
terfeit | Math. 6.24.

1 Ioh.2.15.	*terfeit* loue of him: all *inordinate* loue of ones selfe, or of other creatures.
Rom.16.18.	
Phil.3.19.	
	4 *Hypocriticall trust* in God; *staggering* and *diffidence* in the goodnesse and power of God: *Confidence* in the *helpe* of man.
Iob 31.24.	
Esay 7.12.	
Ierem 17.5.	
Dan.4.27.	5 *Pride, Arrogance,* counterfeit *humility*.
1.King.21.27.	
Psal.78.19.	6 *Impatience*, or murmuring against God.
Mal.3.14.	7 *Desperation*, and *Presumption*.
Ierem.9.23.	
1.Cor.4.7.	

2 COMMANDEMENT.

Thou shalt not make to thy selfe any grauen Image, to bowe downe to it to worship it.

The *Duty* commanded, is,

Phil.2.10.	To giue vnto God *al outward religious worship* of the *body*, as in the first Commandement, we are inioyned to *Honour him in our heart* aboue all.
Rom.14.11.	
Esay 45.23.	

The

to the Sacrament.

The maine sinnes forbidden are.

1 To *adore with the body*, (in a religious manner) any *Image* made with mans hands, whether it be of *Saint* or *Angell*, or *any* creature.

Rom.1.23.
Exod.32.
1 Sam.5.7.
Psal.16.4.
Ephes.5.5.
Col.2.18.

2 To *deuise* any *bodily* worship of God, which he hath not reuealed, and commanded, either plainely, or by deduction and implicitly.

3 COMMANDEMENT.
Thou shalt not take the Name of the Lord thy God in vaine.

The maine *duty* commanded is the praise of the tongue: and it hath six branches.

1 Due honour and reuerence to the *Name* of God.

2 *Inuocation* and Prayer.
3 *Thanksgiuing*.
4 *Confession*, and publication

Psal.50.15.
Ioel 2.12.
Iohn 16.23.
Heb.1.6.
Psal.147.7.
Mat.10.13.

A Preparation

tion of Gods praises.

5 The *glorifying* of his name.

6 *Swearing lawfully* by the Name of God.

The *sinnes* forbidden are:

1 *Want of Reuerence* to the Name of God; *neglect of Prayer, Inuocation, Thanksgiuing, Confession, Praise, and glorifying of God.*

2 All *Banning, Cursing, Blasphemies, Maledictions, imprecations,* wherein the name of God is vsed and prophaned.

3 All *forswearing, false swearing, light* and *common swearing:* all *foolish calling* of God to witnesse, all *rash* vowes.

4 All *Enchantments, Witchcrafts, Sooth-sayings, Diuinations, Exorcisings,* and other *Magicall Superstitions*, which are made by *Wizards* out of the Scripture for the most part.

5 All

Psal. 34. 4.
Deut. 6. 13.
& 10. 20.

Mark. 11. 24.
1. Cor. 11. 23, 24, 25, 27.

Rom. 2. 24.
Math. 5. 34.
Ecclus. 23. 9.

Leuit. 19. 12.
Math. 5. 34.
Psal. 15. 3.
Iam. 5. 12.

Leuit. 29. 6.
Deut. 18. 10.

1. Sam. 28. 7.

to the Sacrament.

5 All *wiles, deceits, cousenages* and *lyes*, broached vnder *pretence* of the *Name* and *Word* of God. Ier 14 15. Ephes.5.4.

4. COMMANDEMENT. *Thou shalt keepe holy the Sabbath day.*

The maine duty commanded, is *glory*, which consists in a religious worshipping of God *in publique*, in the *great congregation*, which is nothing else but our doing *of Seruice to God* in *Common Prayer* and *Thanksgiuing* in the *Church*. And it consisteth in fiue things. Psal.92.1,2,3,4, 5,6.

Heb. 10.25.

1 An *attentiue* hearing and *meditating* of Gods *works*, and his *word* preached. Acts 13. 44. 1 Cor.14.26.

2 A *frequent vse* of the blessed Sacraments. 1 Cor. 11.20. Acts 20.7.

3 *Deeds of piety* to the maintenance of the *Ministers* of 1 Cor.16.1. Galat.6.6.

E Christ,

Christ, and *Almesdeeds* to the *Poore*.

4. *Charitable offices* to our *Neighbours*, in *comforting* the *afflicted*, *visiting* the *sicke*, &c.

Titus 2.10.
Rom. 2.24.

5 A *squaring* of our owne liues and manners according to *right* Christianity.

Sinnes forbidden are.

1 *Absenting* our selues *wilfully* from the *Church*, vpon *Sundays* and other *Holidayes* : or (being present) not to *regard* the *Seruice* that wee ought to tender *there* to God in *publique*; but to come onely to heare a *Sermon*, which is but an *Inferiour end* of comming to Church vpon Holydayes, wherein *God* doth rather *serue* vs, then *wee serue* God.

Col. 3.16.
Psal. 92.
Heb. 10.25.

2 *Contemning* of the *Ministery* of the Word and Sacraments, or any kind of *abuse* of the same.

Mat. 11.16, 17.

3 *Neg-*

to the Sacrament.

   3 *Neglecting* to *heare* or *reade* the *Scriptures*, *intermission* of *prayers*, *deeds* of *Piety*, *Mercy*, and *Charity*.   Luke 4.16.
1 Tim.2.10.
Iames 2.18.

   4 *Intermedling* with *common*, *prophane*, and *ordinary affaires* on those dayes.   Leuit.27.7.8.
Nehem.13.15.
Ier.17.24.

   5 *Bibbings*, *feastings*, *Reuellings*, *Dancings* and *Sportings*, to the *hinderance* of our deuotions, and seruice of God.   Rom.6.19.

So much for the *first Table*. The *second Table* respects our *Neighbour*: and it containeth six Commandements; whereof the *first*, commandeth vs to doe our *Neighbour all the good we can*: the *other* charge vs to doe him no *manner of hurt*.

   Mat.22.39.
Mat.7.12.
Hæc est proximi tota dilectio; vt bonum quod tibi conferri vis, velis & proximo: & malum, quod tibi accidere nolis, nolis & proximo: Prosper. de vit. Contemp. L 3. cap.15.

5. COMMANDEMENT.
Honour thy Father and thy Mother.

   This Commandement tea-
E 2   cheth

cheth the duties of *Superiors* to their *Inferiors*: and of all *Inferiors* to their *Superiors*.

The Duties of *Superiors* to their *Inferiors* are:

First, to embrace them with a *fatherly* affection.

Secondly, as much as in vs lyeth, to *prouide* for their *maintenance* and *education*.

Thirdly, to *defend* them from wrong and violence.

Ephes.6.4.

Fourthly, to *instruct* them in the *feare* and *nurture* of the Lord.

Fiftly, to giue *good example* vnto them by our owne *religious* and *honest* cariage.

Sixtly, to *chastise* and *correct* them for their offences.

The *Duties* of *Inferiors* to *Superiors*, are:

Ephes.6.1,2.
Tobit.4.3.

First, to shew all *filiall loue* vnto them.

Se-

Secondly, to *honour* them inwardly, in *Heart*, by a reuerent estimation of them; and *outwardly*, in *word and gesture*, by bowing to them, and speaking *submissely* and humbly to them.

Thirdly, to yeeld all *willing obedience* to their commands, *so long as they are not crosse to Gods Commandements*.

Fourthly, to *imitate* their vertuous life, and religious conuersation.

Fiftly, in *word and deed* to expresse our *thankfulnesse* vnto them.

Sixtly, to *winke* at their *imperfections*, and to *beare* with their *infirmities*.

The *Sinnes* forbidden *both parties*, are:

First, *want of naturall affection*, and all *impiety* towards any

any, to whom we owe loue and reuerence.

Secondly, euery *neglect* of duty, or an *hypocriticall faining* of the same.

Thirdly, too much *Indulgence* or *ouer-fondnesse*.

Fourthly, *Contempt, Scorne, Stubbornnesse*.

Fiftly, *Ingratitude*.

Sixtly, too much *rigour, seuerity, roughnesse* or *harshnesse* of behauiour.

Seuenthly, *Lightnesse, immodesty, Boasting*.

6. COMMANDEMENT.
Thou shalt not kill.

The *sinnes* here forbidden, are:

First, all manner of *hurt* or violence done to the *person* of our neighbour.

Secondly, *Anger, Hatred, Euill-*

Exod. 21. 24.
Num 25. 7.

Mat. 5. 22.
Hof. 3. 15.

Euill-will, Rancor, desire of Reuenge.   Gal.5.20. Rom.1.29.

Thirdly, *Waywardnesse, Inhumanity, Wrathfull lookes.*   Phil.2.14.16. 13.5. 2 Cor.12.24. Mat.5.22.

Fourthly, *Rayling, Ill words, Insulting prouocations* to anger.   Rom.1.30. Gal.5.15.

Fiftly, *Trechery, Cruelty.*   Rom.12.14.

The *Duties* commanded are:

First, *Humanity*, and an *vnfained* loue of our neighbour.

Secondly, *Beneuolence*, or well-wishing to his person from a *compassionate heart.*

Thirdly, *Meeknesse* and *long suffering, patiently bearing,* and *willingly forgiuing* iniuries.

Fourthly, *affability, gentlenesse,* and al kind of *courteous behauiour.*

7. COMMANDEMENT.

E4   *Thou*

Thou shalt not commit Adultery.

The *sins* forbidden are:

First, all *Lustings* and *Longings in the heart* after the carnall company of our Neighbour.

Secondly, *Immodesty*, the *wanton eye*, the *Whorish forehead*, *Mincing gate*, and *Garish attire*.

3 *Loue-songs, filthy* and *bawdy talking.*

All manner of *vncleannesse*, whether it be with a *single* person, or with a *maried* person, and *how else soeuer.*

The *Duties* commanded, are:

1 *Chastity* of body and mind, whether it bee in the state of *Virginity*, *Mariage*, or *Widowhood.*

2 *Modesty*, adorning our thoughts, words, deeds, gesture, coun-

---

Mat.5.28.

1 Pet.2.14.
Prou 7 13.
Esay 3.

Col.3.8.
Eph.4.29.

Rom.1.32.

Ores, casta legas, ieiunes, otia vites:
Si seruare voles corpora casta Deo.

countenance, attire, gate, conuersation.

3 *Moderation*, and *Temperance* in meate, drinke, sleepe, &c.

8 COMMANDEMENT.

Thou shalt not steale.

Sinnes forbidden are.

1 The *inward greedinesse of the heart*, longing after *wealth*, howsoeuer to be gotten; *Auarice, coueting other mens* riches.

2 All *Fraud, Guile, Deceit, trickes, quirkes*, all *impostures* in bargaines, and contracts, and *selling* of *counterfeit* wares. | Leuit. 19. 11. Amos 8. 5, 6. Deut. 25. 1 Thes. 4. 6.

3 *Vsury* and *Extortion*, or *Oppression*. | Mich. 3. Exo. 22. Pro. 22. Ezech. 18.

4 *Theft, Robbery, Sacriledge, Couzening* of the Country or Common-weale, &c. | Thom. 2. 2, q. 66. Iob 24. 9.

5 *Idlenesse.*

6 *Nigardise* and *Profusion*. | Ezech. 16.

The

The *Duties* commanded are:

1 *Iustitia commutatiua*, Iust and *vpright dealing*, in getting, in buying, and selling.

Prou. 5. 16.
Rom. 12. 13.

2 *Care to saue our Neighbour from Dammage*: *Diligence* in doing the works of our *Calling*.

Heb. 13.
1 Tim 6. 17.

3 *Liberalitie.*
4 *Frugalitie.*

9. COMMANDEMENT.

Thou shalt not beare false witnesse.

Sinnes forbidden are.

Exod. 23. 3.
Psal. 101.
Iob 29.
Leuit. 19. 15.
1 Cor. 6. 10.
1 Cor. 5. 11.

1 All manner of *lying* and *false testimonies*.

2 *Pratling, babling, scurrilitie, slandering, defaming,* and *backbiting*.

Math 15. 19.
1 Cor 13. 4.

3 Sinister *suspition*, rash and wrongfull iudging of our neighbour.

Duties

to the Sacrament.

Duties commanded are.

1 Sincere and *plain meaning* and *speaking*. — Psal.15.3.

2 *Taciturnitie, graue speech*, and a *moderate* vse of the tongue. — 1 Pet.3.10. Iof.2.14.

3 Bearing of a *good opinion*, of our Neighbour, and iudging all things to *the best*.

10 COMMANDEMENT.

Thou shalt not couet.

The *former Commandements* doe forbid the *thoughts* and *desires* of the heart, as well as the *outward Act and Practice*. For God is a *Spirit*, and therefore must be *worshipped in the Spirit*. — Iohn 4.

But the *former* Commandements did condemne the *setled thought* to doe mischiefe: But *this* condemneth euen the very first *inclination and motion to sinne*, though a man doe *neuer* — Rom.7.7.

con.

consent, but *snub* it in the *beginning*.

The *neglect of doing* what we are commanded, is a *sinne* of *Omission*.

The *doing* of that which we are forbidden, is a *Sinne* of *Commission*.

If therefore we shal examine the *face* of our soules by the *Looking-glasse* of the *Law* of God, wee shall finde it strangely *defiled* and deformed with spots and staines; nay, much *defaced* with Byles, Vlcers, and wounds, which cannot choose but wound and *pierce* our *hearts* with sorrow: Especially if wee consider the *party* against *whom* euery sinne, which the law chargeth vs withall, is either *immediately*, or *mediatly* committed; and *secondly*, if wee lay to our hearts the *horrour* of that punishment

nishment whereunto wee are lyable and obnoxious by euery sinne, whether it be of *Omission* or *Commission*.

First then, the *party dishonoured*, and offended by our sinnes, is the *most mighty God*, who *made* our bodies and soules, to the end, that wee with them might (not *dishonour* him by breaking his lawes, but) do him *all honour and seruice all the dayes of our life*. In him, we must consider these *three things* specicially: First, his *wisedome and knowledge*: Secondly, his *Iustice*: Thirdly, his *Power*.

First, his *Wisedome* is such, that no *thing*, no *action*, no *cogitation* that passeth from vs, is hidden from it. Hence it is that Saint *Augustine* saith, *Deus totus oculus, quia omnia videt.* God is *all eye*, because hee seeth and

In Psal. 126.

and beholdeth all things. He is *Scrutator cordis*, the *searcher of the heart*; which is *vnsearchable* to any but onely to him. There he sees what we *loue* or *hate*, or *desire*, and *lust for*, what we *plot* and *deuise*, as well as wee our selues; yea, and *much better*. For no man can tell, *this houre*, vpon what hee shall thinke the next *houre*, or the next *day*: but God *who is about our pathes, and about our beds, doth exactly know all our thoughts long before* that they doe arise in our hearts. For which cause the Wise-man affirmeth, that the all-seeing *eyes of the Lord are ten thousand times clearer then the Sunne*. For the *Sunne* giueth *light* to *others*, but *it selfe* seeth nothing: Our *eye* doth see, but it giueth not *light* to any thing: But the *eye of the Lord* performeth *both*. For it

Ierem. 17.

Psal. 139. 2.

Ecclus 23. 19.

to the Sacrament.

it *giueth light* to euery man: and also seeth in the *most secret parts*, euen *into the secrets of mans heart*. The beames of the *Sunne* cannot reach *so farre*. The *Sunne*, (if it could see) can see but *onely* in the *day time*, & not in the night: when it is with the *Antipodes* it seeth not vs in this *Hemisphere*; and when it is aboue our *Hemisphere*, it cannot see the *Antipodes*: but *God* seeth as well by night as by day. *The Light and the Night to him are both alike.* The *Sunne* beholdeth but only *such* things as are *created* and made: but God seeth *all*: as well things *created*, as *increated*. Of *things created*, the Sunne seeth *such* onely as are *present*; not those which are *past*, or *to come*: but God seeth all; *past*, *present*, and *to come*: *Deo antequam crearentur omnia sunt agnita.*

Iohn 1.9.
Ecclus.23.19.
Psal.44.21.

Psal.139.12.

agnita. Hee knew *all things before they were made.* And for his knowledge of things *to come*; he maketh challenge to al the *Gods* and *Idols* of the Heathen. The *Sunne* can see but onely the *outside* and *surface* of things, not the *inner* parts. But the Lords eyes behold as well the *inside* as the *outside.* For there *is not any creature which is not manifest in his sight*; πάντα δὲ γυμνὰ καὶ τετραχηλισμένα, all things are *naked and open* to his eyes. They are *naked,* and therefore he sees their *outside*: and they are τετραχηλισμένα, *dissected, quartered,* and *cleft asunder* through the back bone; so that he sees their *inside* also. Now then consider, that what sinne so euer thou hast committed, in thought, word, or deede, thou hast done it *before the face of God*, in his sight,

Ecclus. 23.20.

Esay 44.7,8.

Heb. 4.13.

sight, and before his eyes, who did strictly forbid *that very sin*, and will one day (*if thou repent not*) sit as a *Iudge* vpon thee to condemne thee *for it*.

What a reproach and dishonour is it to an *earthly King* to see his subiects before *his owne face* to dare to doe that which he directly prohibited? And is it not a *fearfull prouoking* of the vengeance of God, when hee shall see his seruants dare to do what hee forbade, and that before his eyes, whilest hee stands looking on?

Secondly, his *Iustice* is so strict and seuere, that *without full satisfaction*, it will not suffer any *one sinne* to escape *vnpunished*. The *rebell Angels* sinned but *once*, and yet for that one sinne, *They are reserued in euerlasting chaines under darknesse*

nesse to the iudgment of the great day. *Adam*, in *Paradise*, sinned but once, and yet for that *one sinne*, hee and all his posterity were exiled Paradise, and became subiect to eternall death both of body and soule. If *Dauid* sinne, *Dauid* must smart for his sinne. If the *whole Church* of God doe breake the Law of God, (as it did among the Iewes) the vengeance of God shall breake and bruise them in peeces. (*Lament. Ierem.*) Nay, the *seuerity* of God against sin is *so great*, that if hee find sinne in his *owne Sonne*, his owne son shall die for it. Though *Christ Iesus* did no sinne, yet he *vndertooke* for our sinnes, and God finding *our sinnes* vpon *his owne deare Sonne*, (whom hee loued aboue a *million* of worlds, euen as *dearly as himselfe*) would not spare

Iude verse 6.

Gen. 3.

1 Sam. 2.

spare him, but poured vpon his blessed person that direfull vengeance which no creature in the world was able to beare. So that as the *Iewes* when they saw our Sauiour weepe at *Lazarus* his graue, said, *See how he loued him:* so, if wee looke vpon the *Sonne of God* suffering the fierce wrath of God vpon the *Crosse* for our transgressions, every one of vs may speake vnto his owne soule, and say, See and consider (O my soule) *how extreamly* the Lord thy God hateth sin and iniquity? whose iustice will not be satisfied, till the precious blood of Iesus Christ be poured out as a price for it. And then let vs consider, that *if it be done thus to the green tree, what shall become of the dry?* If the innocent and immaculate Lambe of God, the deare Son of God, was so seuerely punished for sinnes which were *none of his owne?* what shall become *of vs* for our own innumerable, haynous, and horrible sinnes, when the Lord shall enter into iudgement with vs, if wee preuent not his iudgment by timely and vnfained repentance?

Thirdly, his *power* is infinit and incircumscriptible: it hath all things vnder it, and cannot bee *eluded* or resisted by any. For which cause *Mercurius Tresmegistus* was wont to say, that God was an *incomprehensible Sphære*, whose *center* was euerywhere, whose *circumference* was no where. Yet notwithstanding *he* encompasseth and *concludeth* all things within the circuit of his circumference, as *Athenagoras* affirmes [*In legatione pro Christianis.*]. In a circumference, wee know,

hat

to the Sacrament.

that the *further* you goe from the *one side*, the *neerer* you are to *another*. So it is with God: if you flie to heauen, he is there; if to the earth, he is there also; there is no scaping from him or his power; nor is there any withstanding or resisting it. For he is *Dominus Exercituum*, the Lord of *Hoasts* & *Armies*; Lord of all the hoasts of creatures in heauen and earth. Euery creature (euen to the *smallest gnat*, or graine of *dust*) is a *souldier* in pay with God, & hath its weapons not onely ~~offensiue~~ *defensiue*, *ad muniendum*, to defend his seruants, but also ~~defensiue~~ *offensiue*, *ad puniendum* to punish his enemies. If hee command, the *meanest* of his creatures will not feare to strike the *proudest* of the sons of men, as they did *Pharaoh*. Mans power may not stand in any com-

F 3 parison

A Preparation

parison with *Gods Almightinesse*. Therefore take heed, *Horrendum est incidere in manus Dei viuentis: It is a dreadfull thing to fall into the hands of the liuing God*. *Mans power* may be resisted, by an *equal* strength, *Gods* cannot: the power of a *King* may be eluded, by *fleeing* away. But *whither shall I flee from thy presence*, sayth the Psalmist.

Besides, a *King* by his power may torment and punish the *body of a traytor*, or other malefactor; but he cannot reach his *soule*: but God can cast both *body* and *soule* into Hell fire, and all the *Kings* on Earth, or *Angels in heauen*, shall not be able to fetch them backe againe. In the very *act* of *thy sinne* hee is able to destroy both thy body and thy soule, and to *snatch thee*

Hebr. 12.

Psal. 139.

Psal. 50. last.

thee away, so that there shall bee none to deliuer thee.

Then in the *second* place, we should do wel to consider what *punishment* is due to vs for euery sinne; that is, eternall death and destruction of body & soule in hell fire. *The wages of sinne is death. Rom. 6. vlt.* A *thousand* sinnes, a *thousand* deaths in hell (except wee doe truely repent of them before wee part hence.) This punishment is *euery impenitent person*, young and old, Prince and Peasant, to expect as *certainly* as God is God. We are not therefore to thinke *sleightly* of this punishment, but to lay it to our *hearts*, and *dwell* vpon the meditation of it, that it may *worke* vpon our soules. For it is not any slight and superficiall *flea-biting*; but *so dreadful* and horrible, that *those mi-*

miserable *tormented spirits*, which doe now feele it, are not able by any meanes to vtter and *expresse* the extremity thereof. For as the *ioyes and pleasures* which God hath treasured vp for such as loue him, are such, as neuer eye saw, nor eare heard, nor heart is able to conceiue: So the *punishments and torments*, reserued for vnrepentant persons in Hell, are such, as no *eye euer saw*, no *eare euer heard*, nor *any heart of mortall man was able to conceiue* the *number*, or the *intolerable bitternesse and sharpnesse of them*. All other punishments are *particular*, afflicting some *one* sense or other; *these* are *vniuersall* & generall, tormenting *euery part and ioynt of the body, euery power* and *faculty* of the soule, with a paine *peculiar* and *appropriate*

priate vnto it. *Other* paines may be *auoyded* by flight: but when a man is *bound hand and foot*, how can he flee or runne from them? others, haue some *intermißion*; these are *perpetuall, continuall, without interruption.* If they haue no *intermißion* yet there may bee some *mitigation* and lessening of them, but here the *tormentors* neuer are *weary*, nor the fire *neuer flakes*, but burneth hotter and hotter: other paines (if extreame) in time will *end vs* & kill vs: *these* shall *euer torment* thee, but neuer *consume* thee: euer *torture* thee, but neuer *kill* thee *out-right*. There is but *one good* thing that a damned ghost hath left him, & that is *immortality*; and yet *that* shal but adde to his miseries, & augment his sorrowes. The *fire in this place neuer goeth out*: and

that

that it may *neuer cease* to burne the vngodly, behold, *a Riuer of Brimstone continually running into it*, and *the breath of the euerlasting GOD blowing vpon it to keepe it burning*. And certainly no man is *so neere* these torments as *he* that *least thinkes* on them; and *none* more likely to escape Hell, then *he* that in this world doth euery day, in his priuate Meditations, *take a turne or two in Hell*.

Now surely, if wee lay but *these things* together, and apply them to our selues (me thinkes) we cannot choose but haue our *hearts bruised* and broken with griefe and sorrow. Sorrow of *Attrition* at the least, if not sorrow of *Contrition*: sorrow of *Attrition* is when we grieue for *feare of punishment*, which the Law of God doth threaten to the

the transgressors thereof. *[T]his*, by some, is called a *legall* or *seruile sorrow*, which is conceiued when wee come to a sight and knowledge of our sinnes by the Law: and, *from thence*, come to consider the *penaltie* and κατάκριμα, which by reason of our sinne, wee are lyable vnto. Sorrow of *Contrition* is when we grieue for *sinne, as it is sinne;* That is, as it is a *dishonouring* of our gracious God. This, by some, is called *an Euangelical*, or *filiall sorrow* And, of the *twaine, this latter* sorrow is the *better.* And yet the sorrow of *Attrition* is not to be discommended, or refused: because it may serue as *pædagogus ad Christum*, to be a *Schoole-master to lead vs to Christ*, and as a meanes to bring vs to true *Euangelical* and godly sorrow, which wee call the sorrow

Rom. 3.

sorrow of *Contrition*, whereby wee doe grieue and lament for *no kinde of thing* so much, as that by our sinnes, we haue lost the *fauour of God*, and comfort of his *blessed Spirit*.

In this *Contrition*, wee must looke, that our sorrow be *heartie, intire, speedy*, and that it *hold out* to the last. For *Contrition* is the beginning of *Conuersion*, and these foure things are requisit in both.

First, our godly sorrow must be from *within*, from the very *heart*; not in outward *shew* onely; as *hanging downe the head like a bul-rush* for a day; for that is *hypocriticall*, and odious to God. This is but cleansing the *outside of the Platter*, which we know, our *Sauiour* reproued in the *Pharisees*. But true godly sorrow must come from the heart

Math. 23. 25.

heart and the Spirit. *The sacrifices of God are a contrite spirit, a contrite and broken heart, O God, thou wilt not despise.* Therefore the Prophet *Ioel* tels vs that if we will truely repent and turne to the Lord, wee must *rent our hearts.* Saint *Paul* calleth sinne σκόλοψ, and *some* say that σκόλοψ doth signifie the *head of a barbed Arrow.* If the *smooth* head of an *Arrow* enter our *flesh*, it may bee pulled out, and healed *without any great paine or difficulty*: but a *Barbed-head*, being once gotten into the flesh, cannot be *pulled out*, but with great paine, for it *teares the flesh round about*, and causeth much paine. *Such* is *sinne*, it is shot and *fastened* into our hearts, and we cannot get it out, except wee *rent and teare the heart in pieces* with sorrow and compunction for the

Psal. 51. 17.

Ioel 2. 13.
2 Cor. 12. 7.

the same. For, *peccata extrinsecus radere, & non intrinsecus eradicare, fictio est* (saith *Bernard* Sermon 2. *de Assumptione Mariæ*) *To shaue sinne off from our outward liues, and not to root them quite out of the heart, is a meere mockery.*

Secondly, this Contrition and godly sorrow must bee *intire, with all the heart.* Many can bee content to lament and sorrow *some* sinnes, but *other darling* sinnes, they *nouzle* and make much of: here the sorrow is *lame* and *maimed*, and not pleasing to God, nor profitable to our owne Soules. *One Serpent* may sting a man to *death*: and one sinne, harboured in thy bosome, and not cast out by repentance will sting thy Soule to eternall death.

Thirdly, this godly sorrow must

must *bee speedy*, without delay. For hee, which hath promised *mercy to the contrite* and broken heart, hath not promised thee *one day* or houres space of life to breake and bruise thine heart in. God will not bee shifted off with excuses and delayes. For to giue our *prime dayes* of our flowring youth and lustihead to the *pleasures* of sinne, and the *Dogge-dayes* of our doting and decrepit age to grieue and sorrow for our sinnes, what is it but to offer vp our *Wine to Satan*, and to giue the *Lees and dregs* to God?

Fourthly, it must *hold out* to the last; for hee that *continueth to the end shall be saued*. Otherwise if our *Contrition* bee for a *spurt*, or take vs like a *fit* of an Ague, it is nothing worth. God would haue *those* that mourne for

Greenh.

A Preparation

for their sins marked with the signe *Thau*. As ωμέγα, is the *last letter* of the *Greeke*; so is *Tau* the last of the *Hebrew Alphabet*. To signifie, that our *mourning and sorrow for sinnes should bee constant, and perseuering to the very last*.

This godly sorrow, thus qualified, will worke in vs *repentance not to be repented of*. Nay, such a sorrow will bring *ioy and comfort* to our soules; *Lacrymæ pœnitentium vinum sunt Angelorum*, saith deuout Saint Bernard. *The teares of the penitent, are the Wine of the Angels:* it makes them *glad and merry* at the heart. Nay, these sorrowfull teares of repentant sinners, are *wine* to the *penitents themselues*: for nothing doth more *reioyce and glad* the soule of a *Penitent*, then *Compunction* and *contrition* for

Ezekiel 9.4.

2 Cor. 7.10.

Luke 15.10.

for his sinnes. O how sweet a thing it is, at the feet of Iesus, to stand weeping; to water them with teares, to dry them with sighs, and to kisse them with our mouthes! No man but he that hath felt and *experienced* it, can *truely vnderstand it*.

Some, in this case, are much *mistaken*: for generally, men imagine that *Repentance* is nothing else but a *godly sorrow* for sinne committed. But Saint *Paul* had studied the case *thorowly*; and he teacheth vs farre *otherwise*: namely, that *Repentance* and godly sorrow do *differ* one from another, as the *Cause* differeth from the *Effect*. For *godly sorrow* (saith hee) *causeth or worketh repentance*. So that Repentance is an *effect*, a *worke*, or *fruit* of godly sorrow: and *godly sorrow* is the *cause* of repentance.

Lapid.

G

A Preparation

tance. Wherefore they cannot be *one* and the *selfe-same* thing: for, *Nihil est causa suiipsius.* Nothing is cause of it selfe.

Saint *Paul* tels vs that *Repentance* is another manner of matter, and consists of, or *rather* declareth it selfe by *seuen effects* or fruits. An *Inuentory* whereof the Apostle deliuereth vnto vs: *For, behold this godly sorrow, what great carefulnesse it hath wrought in you?* Yea, what *Apologie, or defence?* Yea, *what Indignation?* Yea, *what feare? yea, what earnest desire?* Yea, *what Zeale, or emulation?* Yea, *what reuenge, or punishment.*

These bee the *seuen* fruits of *true contrition,* or parts of the *body* of Repentance; and according to *these,* we are to examine our consciences, to see whether our Repentance bee sound, or no.

Lapid. in loc.

Bucan. in locis.
Lapid. in 2 Cor. 7.

2 Cor.7.1 .

no. For in the *exercise* of true Repentance, not any one *particular part* alone, but the *whole man* is to be set on work: namely, both the *vnderstanding part*, and the *affections*, and the *body*.

The *vnderstanding part* must exercise it selfe in *carefulnesse*, and *Apologie*.

The *affections* are to be exercised in *Indignation, Feare, Desire, and Emulation*.

The *body*, in *reuenge* and *punishment*.

These are the seuen *fruits meet for Repentance*, which *Iohn* the *Baptist* doth so earnestly call for. These are they, saith *Bullinger*, which giue *life and spirit to Repentance*, without which *no repentance is perfect* and compleate. And this place of the Apostle doth more rightly and *fully* teach vs to distin- guish

Matth. 3.

guish betwixt *true* repentance and *false*, then all the *Tractates* and *Volumes* of the *Schoolemen* written vpon this Argument.

First then, to *assure* our *consciences* that our *Repentance* is sound, there is required in vs a studious *carefulnesse*, to auoid sinnes to come, and a sollicitous *thought-fulnesse* diligently to performe those good workes which the law of God doth enioyne vs. For so long as *our hearts are not stung* with compunction and sorrow for our sinnes past, and that wee haue little feeling of the same, wee *slumber away* our liues in carelesse securitie, not regarding which end goes forward; nor thinking much of Heauen, or Hell, or any matter that pertaines to another life.

This is the *first* part of the Body

Caluin in Loc.

dy of repentance, and it belongs to the *superiour* part of the soule, the *vnderstanding*.

The *second* Act of Repentance, which pertaineth to the *vnderstanding* part, is *Apologie*, or *Defence*. Where the Apostles meaning is not, that a man should stand to iustifie or defend his sinnes. (For *he that hideth or excuseth his sinne shall not prosper*) which is an Act cleane contrary to Repentance: but that a Christian by *humble confession of his faults, heartily* crauing of pardon vpon promise of future amendment, should make a iust *Apologie* for himselfe, that *his* godly sorrow is sincere and vnfained. For ἀπολογία doth signifie *not onely to excuse* and iustifie ones selfe from a *crime* obiected against him; but also, *when a man is guilty*, to acknowledge & *confesse*

Prou. 28.

fesse his fault, crauing pardon for the same. And in this later sense Saint *Paul* vseth this word, ἀπολογία. *Quæ magis deprecatione constat, quàm depulsione Criminum.* As a *child* hauing done a *shrewd* turne, doth not stand in *defence* thereof before his *Father*; but humbly confessing and acknowledging it, protesting that he will doe no more so, doth, *in a sort, excuse* himselfe, and makes it cleare that he is *heartily sory* that he hath done amisse. And *this* kinde of *Apologie*, or confessing our sins with sorrow before God, is so necessarie, that without it, *no mans sinnes shall euer bee forgiuen.* But *if wee confesse our sinnes, God is faithfull and iust to forgiue vs our sinnes, and to cleanse vs from all our wickednesse.* But this confession must bee made to God; without

Chemnit. Ex. part. 4.

Prou. 28.

without which no sinne is forgiuen: As *Augustine* teacheth. The Papists out of this place (because ἐξομολόγησις in some Copies is vsed in stead of Ἀπολογία) would faine inforce Auricular Confession: but howsoeuer that ἐξομολόγησις bee another matter; yet Saint *Austin* hath these words (as they are alledged.) *What haue I to doe with men, that they should heare my confession, as though they were able to heale my diseases? A sort of men curious to know another mans life; and slothfull to correct and amend their owne; Why doe they seeke to heare of mee what I am, which will not heare of Thee, what they are? And how can they tell when they heare by me of my selfe, whether I tell the Truth, or not; sith no mortall man knoweth what is in Man, but the Spirit*

Epist. 30. ad Iulian. Comitem & Hom. 2. Anglic. de pænit.

L. b. Conf. 10. cap. 3.

Hom. Aug. 2. de pœnitent.

which is in *Man*? *Augustine* would not haue written *thus*, if *Auricular Confession* had beene vsed in *his time*.

These two former Acts belong to the *vnderstanding* or *superiour part* of the Soule. The *affections* are charged with foure things. (viz.) *Indignation, Feare, Desire, Emulation*, or *Zeale*.

Indignation hath respect to sinnes *past*: *Feare* hath regard of sinnes *to come*: *Desire* hath reference to *good things*: *Emulation* is in respect of *good persons*.

The *third* then, of these seuen, is *Indignation*; which is an affection of *Anger*; and doth *most properly* belong to Repentance. For when wee consider *whom*, and vpon *what* slight *occasion*, we haue offended by our sinnes; and *what indignity* wee haue

haue done to *so good* & *so great* a *Maiestie*, and to *our selues* also (who were made after *his Image*) we cannot choose but be enflamed with *anger* and indignation not onely against the *sinne* committed, but also against *our selues* who did commit it. We see deuout and zealous persons, when they behold God offended, are *often* moued to *anger* and indignation against the *parties offending* : or *rather* not *so much* against the *persons*, as against their *sinnes*. Now, this *affection* of *indignation* is farre more vehement and strong then that of sorrow.

The *first step*, to repentance, is to grieue and bee displeased with our selues for displeasing God: the *next* is to be so *infired* with *anger* against our selues, that wee neuer cease, but *instantly*

stantly do vrge vpon our selues, till our consciences doe feele an *inward and serious compunction*, and our hearts bee pricked for the same.

The fourth is *feare to offend* God by our sins hereafter. For as the *contempt* of God is the cause of sinne, so to *feare* and tremble at his *presence* and *word* is a cause of righteousnesse. And surely *they* cannot choose but feare to offend God, who haue a *liuely sense* and feeling of their sinnes past, and doe *vnfainedly beleeue* that hee will (like a iust Iudge) render vengeance to the vngodly, of al the wicked deeds which they haue vngodly committed.

The fift is *desire* to please God in all things: when we can say with *Dauid*, O that my wayes were so direct, that I might keepe thy

thy Statutes. I haue as great delight in the way of thy Testimonies, as in all riches, &c.

The sixt is an *holy emulation of good persons.* In striuing to match them in graces and vertues, and (if it be possible) to ouer-match them.

The seuenth is *reuenge* or punishment: which is the very *perfection* or *complement* of repentance: without which reuenge, *non agitur sed fingitur pœnitentia,* repentance is no repentance but hypocrisie. This ἐκδίκησις is by *Sozomen* termed δίκη τιμωρίας ἢ ἐπιτιμίας: *a sentencing of a mulct or punishment vpon our selues for our sinnes. For what we spake of indignation must be extended to this taking of reuenge* vpon our selues: for, by *doing this,* we doe preuent the iudgement of God; as Saint *Paul* tea-

1 Cor.11.31.

A Preparation

teacheth; *If we would iudge our selues, we should not be iudged of the Lord.* After sitting in iudgement vpon our selues, we must proceed to *sentence*: for this ἐνδίκιον, is a *giuing of sentence* against our selues, according to the *nature* and *quality* of our offences. And after *sentence*, we must not stay till we haue done *execution*, & reuenged, punished, and corrected our selues for our sinnes.

For this *reuenge* is the *highest degree*, and the very perfection of repentance: and so is confessed to bee, not onely by the Fathers and Schoolemen, but also by Master *Caluin* himselfe; who speaking of these fruits of repentance, saith; *Postrema est vindicta; quò enim seueriores in nos sumus & acriore censurâ quæstionem habemus de peccatis nostris, eò sperare debemus*

Marginalia:
1 Cor. 11. 31.
Calv. instit. l. 3. Sect. 16.

bemus magis propitium ac misericordem Dominū. Et certè fieri non potest, quin anima diuini judicij horrore perculsa, partes vltionis, in exigendâ de se pœnâ occupet. The last of these is reuenge; for the more seuere that we are against our selues, and the sharper censure we passe against our sins, so much the more gracious and mercifull are wee to hope to find the Lord vnto vs. And certainly it cannot be chosen, but that the soule which is smitten with horrour of Gods iudgement, should take on it selfe the task of reuenge in exacting punishment vpon it selfe. For, in the very *name* of *penitence*, pain and punishment is included. *Pœnitentia, quasi pœna tenentia.* So that where we *put not* our selues to *paine* and *punishment*, there *is no penitence*.

Vide Aujan.

This

This punishment or reuenge must be *according to the nature of the sinnes. Spirituall sinnes,* (as pride, contempt of God, enuy, wrath, desire of reuenge, inordinate lusts & desires) must be punished *by spirituall castigations:* as by restraining and tying the *mind* to meditate vpon the *day of death,* the *dreadfull iudgement,* the neuer-ending *torments of hell;* by studying to esteem euery man *better* then our selues; to be *patient;* to *put vp* wrongs; *to set our desires on things that are aboue, & not on the things on earth.*

Carnall sinnes must bee punished by *subduing* and beating downe the *flesh. Castigo corpus meum.* The *flesh* desireth *dainty* fare, and sometimes to exceed in them. This must be punished with abstinence and fasting. And

Col. 3. 2.

2.

1 Cor. 9. 25.

And this fasting is of three sorts:

A toto; from all kind of sustenance.

A tanto; from so many meales as we are wont.

A tali; from such exquisit dainties.

If it be possible (without *endangering our health*) we must abstaine from *all kind of sustenance*, as *Dauid* did. And the *Niniuites*, who layd a punishment vpon *themselues*, and gaue charge that neither *man nor beast, bullocke nor sheepe, should tast any thing at all, neither feed, nor drinke water.*

2 Sam. 12. 17.

Ionah 3. 7.

But if wee cannot (without preiudice to our health) abstain *à toto*, from all manner of food; yet are we to abstaine *à tanto*; from *so much*, from so many meales: as, if we haue vsed *two*,

now

now to vse but *one*, and *that a sparing one* too, onely to keepe life and soule together, as wee say.

But if we cannot (with health) abstaine from so many meales; yet wee are to abstaine *à tali*; from *such dainties and delicates* whereby wee may either *pamper our flesh*, or be prouoked to sinne. So *Daniel* when hee was in heauinesse three weekes of dayes, *hee did eate no pleasant bread all that while*. So in *ancient times* they had but *one* meale, viz. a *supper*; and it was *pura & sine animalibus cœna*: no *fleshmeat*, but a thin supper, perhaps of hearbs, which belike *Tertullian* speaketh of, *pastum & potum pura nosse, non ventris sed animæ causâ*.

The *flesh* desires fine & *braue apparell*. This *Dauid* punished, by

Acts 10. 13.

Dan. 10. 2. 3.

Rom. 14. 2.

De pœnitent. cap. 9.

by putting on *sackcloath*: and the *King of Niniueh* put on sackcloath, and *sate in ashes*. So in *Tertullians* time the penitents did *sacco & cilicio incubare*. This wee must chastise by wearing *courser rayment*.

2 Sam. 12.
Ion. 3.6.
De pænit.c.9.

The *flesh* would haue ease & *lye soft*. This wee must punish with *Dauid*, by lying *hard*, as vpon the bare ground.

The *body* desireth *sleepe in excesse*: which must bee punished with *watching*: and if wee cannot *watch* the *whole night*, (as nicest persons can doe *at dice*, and *drabs*, and *drinke*) yet wee must force our selues *at least* to watch *one houre*; but then it must be *with me*: that is, with Christ: my meaning is, *that houre which we force our selues to watch*, must be spent in *prayer* and *other holy exercises*, and reli-

2 Sam. 12.16.
Mat. 26.40.

religious meditations.

The *flesh* lusteth to enioy a *beautifull* person: This must be punished by *making a couenant with our eyes, not to thinke vpon a woman.*

Worldly sinnes are, Ambition, Couetousnesse, thirst after the earthly commodities of this life. These must bee punished by *the purse. First*, by making *restitution* of whatsoeuer wee haue gotten contrary to the Law of God. *Secondly*, by being *bountifull* in deeds of *Piety* to the *Ministers of God,* and to the *House* of God. *Thirdly*, in being beneficiall and *open-handed*, in deeds of *mercy* to the poore. Thus are wee to *take reuenge* vpon our sinnes, that wee may escape the vengeance of God another Day.

Wee must chastice our selues for

Iob 31.

for the sinnes *fore-passed* by crucifying and *killing* them in vs; and, *not staying there*, wee must practise vertues *contrary to those* vices whereunto wee had formerly addicted our selues. *This* was the *repentance* which the old *Prophets* taught the *Church of God* in their dayes. If *a man be iust, and doe that which is lawfull and right, and hath not eaten vpon the Mountaines, nor lift vp his eyes to Idols, nor defiled his neighbours wife; nor hath oppressed any: but hath restored the pledge, and hath not spoiled by violence, but hath giuen his bread to the hungry, and hath couered the naked with a Garment; and hath not giuen forth vpon Vsury, neither hath taken any encrease, but hath withdrawne his hand from iniquitie, and hath executed true iudgement betweene man and man;*

Ezech. 18. 5, 6, 7, 8, 9.

man; and hath walked in my Statutes, and kept my iudgements to deale truely: He is iust, hee shall surely liue, saith the Lord God. Wee must not onely *cast away* all our former transgressions, whereby we haue transgressed; but make vs *new hearts*, and *new spirits*. Not only *eschew euill, but doe good*. Not onely put off the old man, but put on the New Man. Which doing of good, and putting on the new man, or walking in the commandements of God is by the New-writers called *New Obedience*. The *leauing* of our sinnes, and *pulling them vp by the Roots* out of our hearts, is called by them, according to Scripture phrase, *Mortification*. The doing of godly and righteous workes prescribed in Gods Law, they tearme *viuification*. And *these* two they make the

two

Ezech.18.31.
Psal.34.14
Col.3.9,10.

two *generall parts* of Repentance; vnder *which* all the rest are comprised.

It is not a short *momentany* sorrow (as, *Lord haue mercy vpon me, and I will doe no more so*) that will *assure* our hearts of *Remission*. King *Dauid* could not satisfie himselfe with *that*; till he had *humbled his soule* with fasting in sackcloth and ashes, and *chastised* himselfe in bitternesse of his soule, whereof the *one and fiftieth Psalme* is a Monument vnto the worlds end. *Peter* was not at *quiet* with himselfe, till hee had *by going out of* company *for shame*, called himselfe to a *seuere account*, and for *griefe* of heart shed *bitter teares*. *Mary Magdalen* thought it *not enough* for her wanton life, till shee had *wreaked and reuenged* her selfe of *euery* thing, shee be-

fore

fore had abused to sinne. Till *those* wanton *eyes*, which before had been glancing in the *corners* of the world, were turned into *Fountaines* of brinish *teares* to wash the *feet* of our blessed Sauiour; till *that hayre*, which before shee had twined into *Venus net* to catch *Salomons foole* withall, was made a *Towell* to wipe *those surbaited* feete which her teares had bathed. *Thus* did the *penitent Saints of God revenge* themselues on themselues for offending so *gracious* a God. For were it not for *these outward signes* and fruits of sorrow, how should we know our sorrow to be *deepe* and *hearty*?

If *any worldly matter* cause sorrow, that *sorrow* presently brings forth *these effects*; namely, wee *looke heauily, withdraw* our selues from company, *forsake*

sake our meat, *shead* teares, *beat* our breasts: And if *true penitent* forrow for sinne did touch vs *at the heart*, would it not shew it selfe *in these* and the *like* effects? Surely, if it doe not manifest it selfe in this sort, it is but a *slight* and *superficiall* sorrow: and if *slight* and *superficiall* (I feare me) not *sufficient*; for our *sinnes* be neither *slight* nor *superficiall*. If the *children* of the Bride-chamber did fast for sorow, when the Bridegroome was *taken* away: shall wee by sinne *driue away* our *Bridegroome Christ*, and shall not *wee* fast for sorrow? We will *weepe* ouer the *body* of a deare friend, out of which the *soule* is gone: and shall not wee weepe ouer a *dead Soule*, out of which *God is gone*? and yet by *weeping* wee may get *God* into the *Soule* a-
gaine:

gaine: but wee shall neuer get the *Soule* into the *body* againe.

Repentance therefore (if it be *sound* and *sincere*) is a *bitter Passion*, and will so deepely touch vs at the *heart*, that wee shall haue very *small* lift euer to commit the *same sinnes* againe, for which we haue *once* seriously repented. We cannot reade in the *booke of God* of any *one* Saint of God, which repented of *any one sinne*, and euer committed the *same* againe. *Dauid* did not returne *with the Dogge vnto his vomit*; nor *Mary Magdalen*, with the Sow, vnto her wallowing in the myre. For they knew well enough that *Irrisor est, & non pænitens, qui adhuc agit quod pæniteat, nec videtur Deum poscere sub ditus, sed subsannare superbus*; as *Isidore* saith. Hee is a

mocker

mocker of God, and no true *penitent*, which *still* doth that whereof hee ought to repent; nor doth he seeme in *humility* to *implore Gods mercy*; but in *pride* and *arrogance* to *scoffe at his iustice* and power. To which agreeth that of *Clemens Alexandrinus Stromat. 2.* δόκησις μετανοίας ἡ μετανοία, τὸ πολλάκις αἰτεῖσθαι συγγνώμην ἐφ' οἷς πλημμελοῦμεν πολλάκις, *It is but a Repentance in shew onely, and no repentance in truth, often to beg pardon of those sins, in which we doe often transgresse.* I haue stayed the longer vpon *this point*, because as there is no *saluation without repentance*, so neither is there any profitable *accesse* to the *Lords Table* without it. But the Law is not onely a *Looking-glasse*, to shew vs the staines and spots of our sinnes, but also our

Schoole-

Schoolemaster to bring vs to Christ, to the Gospell.

Gal. 3. 24.

Therefore I proceed now to the *second matter*, concerning which wee are to make our examination, and that is *Faith*, and it consisteth of two things; *knowledge* and *application*.

Knowledge.

Touching Knowledge; euery Communicant is bound to know three *generall points* of Christian Religion.

These, (as also the *Summe* of all, which *Christians* are *bound to beleeue*) are contained in the *Creed*; which consisteth of three generall parts. The first part whereof concerneth *God the Father*; the second, *God the Sonne*; the third, *God the Holy Ghost*.

Of Christ.

The *Maine part* of the Creed is that which concerneth *Iesus Christ*. Wherein I am taught to to beleeue *with my heart*, That Iesus Christ is *very God*, begotten of the *Father* from all eternity, *before all worlds* ; and the *same* Christ is *True Man*, borne of *Mary* the Virgin: This *God-Man*, and *Man-God* is my *Lord*, who (when I was vtterly perished and damned) *redeemed* me from *Death*, and from the *power of Satan* ; not with *gold* or *siluer*, but with his owne holy & *precious blood*, and by his *vndeserued death* and *passion* : that *I* might bee *his owne*, & might liue in his *kingdome*, and serue *Him* without *seruile feare*, in perpetuall holinesse and righteousnesse of life; euen as hee *rose* from the *dead*, and now *liueth* and reigneth for euer. I beleeue that there is no *Saluation* but *by him onely* ; no *fruition* of God, but through him.

A Preparation

him. Hee purchased Saluation and Redemption, *not for me only, but for the whole world.*

But the *Benefit* of Redemption is an *vniuersall benefit*, and belongeth to *all mankind*; yet *all mankind* are not *partakers* of it. *None* doe (*ordinarily*) partake of it, but such as haue it passed vnto them *vnder Seale*. The *Seales* which God vseth to *apply vnto me* in particular, that which Christ wrought for *all the world* in generall, are the *two Sacraments*: *Baptisme*, and the *Communion* of Christs body and blood. And *here* comes in the *necessity* of Faith, concerning the Sacraments: for *they* are *both* of them, *Sacramenta Fidei*, Sacraments of Faith : *so called* by the Fathers ; because the *mysteries* in them contained are *not* to be *iudged* by our *Senses,*

---

1 Iohn 2.2.

Of the Sacrament.

ses, nor *discussed* by *Reason*, but to be *apprehended* and receiued *by Faith onely*.

In *both* the Sacraments, there be *two things* to be considered: there is an *earthly thing* which we see and feele with our *outward Senses*; and there is an *heauenly and spirituall thing or grace*, which we *cannot see*, but by *Faith*. *Both* these *parts* are inseparably vnited, and cannot be separated one from another. He that is *rightly fitted* for the receiuing of the Sacrament, doth *receiue both these parts together*, namely, the *earthly* with the *heauenly*, and the *heauenly* with the *earthly*, which are so *inseparably* conioyned by God (in a *Sacramentall vnion*) that he that goeth about to separate them, must needs *runne* himselfe vpon a *curse*.

But

But as wee are *not to diuide* and disioine one part from another, so we must take heed, that we doe *not confound* them one with another, but keepe them *distinct*. As for example. We know that *in the Person* of our Sauiour Christ there are *two seuerall Natures*, viz. the *Godhead* and the *Manhood*. The Nature of *Man* is not the Nature of *God*; nor is the Nature of *God*, the Nature of *Man*. The *one* is not turned into the *other*; neither are they *blended* and *mingled* one Nature with the other; but both remaine *distinct* in the same person: yet are they so *indissolubly vnited* (by *personall vnion*) that *Death* was not able to sunder or separate them. For howsoeuer (*at the death of Christ*) his *Soule* was separated from his *Bodie*, and

and his *Bodie* sundered from his *Soule*; yet euen *when hee lay in the graue, both* the parts of his Humane Nature, *Body* and *Soule*, were as *neerely* vnited to his *Godhead*, as they were at his *Birth*, or *are now* in heauen.

So (to restraine my speech to the Communion) There are *two distinct* and seuerall things in the Sacrament; an *Earthly*, as Bread and Wine: and an *Heauenly*; *sc.* The Body and Blood of Christ. The *Body* of Christ is not turned into the *Bread*, neither is *Bread* turned into the body of Christ. Nor is the *one* blended or mingled with *the other*; but *both* remaine *distinct* in the *same* Sacrament: yet (though they bee in themselues distinct) they are so inseparably conioyned together (*by Sacramentall and mysticall vnion*) that he he that doth receiue *the one rightly*, doth also *necessarily* receiue the *other*.

And as by *vertue* of the *personall union* of the two natures in Christ, it commeth to passe, that there is a *Communication of* properties; by reason whereof that which *properly* belongs to *one* Nature, is attributed to *the other*, as *God is said to bee borne*, and *to dye*: and *the Sonne of Man is said to bee in Heauen, when hee was on Earth*. *God* is (by reason hereof) said to bee *Man*; and *Man* to be *God*, and that *really*, and *truely*.

So, by *vertue* of the *Sacramentall union*, that is betwixt the *hallowed bread*, and the *body* of Christ in the Sacrament: the *Bread* is truely called the *Body* of Christ, and the *bodie* of Christ the *bread*.

The

Iohn 3.13.

to the Sacrament.

The *fruit* of this Sacrament, is the *participation of the Body and Blood of Christ*. There is *no one sentence* of holy Scripture which saith that we cannot, by this Sacrament, be made partakers of Christ his Bodie and Blood, except *they* be first *materially contained* in the *consecrated Elements* of Bread and Wine; or the *Bread* and *Wine* bee *substantially* changed, the one into the *Body*, the other into the *blood* of Christ. *This is my body*, *This is my blood*; are words of *promise*: wee doe *beleeue* that God is *faithfull* and *true* of his word, and doth performe what hee doth promise; Albeit wee doe not vnderstand the *manner how*: nor dare *prescribe* vnto him the manner, *which way* hee shall make it *his body* to vs, either by *Transub-*

I *stantiating*

ſtantiating or Conſubſtantiating it, or elſe wee *will not beleeue him.*

Still remember, that it is a *Sacrament of Faith*, and *Faith* hath relation to a *word of promiſe*. The *word* of promiſe is: *This is my body.* This *word* I beleeue to be *true*, becauſe *God* ſpake it, who cannot *poſsibly lye. This promiſe* I know certainly that *God* will *performe*, (in *making it* his Body *to mee*) becauſe *God* is *faithfull* in performing his promiſe. I confeſſe I doe not know *which way*, or *after what manner* hee will, or doth performe it: becauſe *hee* hath *not ſhewed me.*

If I knew the *manner how* God did make it his Body, then the Sacrament were to mee as matter *rather of Reaſon* and Knowledge, then a *Myſterie of Faith*

Faith and beliefe: *I beleeue* that Christ was conceiued in *the wombe* of *Mary, a pure Virgin*, which neuer knew Man: but if you aske mee *the manner how?* I confesse, *I know not*: and if I *knew* the *manner* how; then *that Article* of Christs Conception, were to *mee* rather a matter of *Knowledge*, then an Article of *faith*.

Moreouer, seeing these words (This is my body) are *words of Promise*: and seeing that both *Protestants*, and *Lutherans*, and *Papists* doe *all agree*, that *by the Sacrament*, Christ doth *really* and *truely* perform in vs his *promise*; what doth it profit vs to know whether hee doth it by *Consubstantiation*, or *Transubstantiation*, or *some other way*, best knowne to himselfe? which is a *thing* which

A Preparation

which can *no wayes* either further vs, or hinder vs, howsoeuer it stand.

Therefore I aduise you to follow the counsell of a most iudicious, and exquisite Diuine, Master *Hooker*, who willeth you to take that wherein *all sides* (both Protestants, and Papists, and Lutherans) *do agree and consent*: and then consider *by it selfe*, what cause there is, why *the rest in question* should not rather bee *reiected* as superfluous, then *vrged* as necessary It is on *all sides* confest.

First, that the Sacrament is a *True* and *Reall participation* of Christ, who thereby imparteth not onely *Totum sui*, but *Totum se*, Himselfe wholly, euen his whole entire person, as a *Mysticall head* vnto euery Soule that receiueth him: and that euery

Eccl. Polit. lib. 5.

to the Sacrament.

every such Receiuer doth *incorporate, or vnite himselfe to Christ, as a Mysticall member* of *him*: yea, and as a *fellow member* of *all true Christian Soules, liuing* on earth, *or triumphing* in heauen.

Secondly, it is also agreed on; That to whom the *person of Christ* is thus communicated, *to them* he giueth (by the same Sacrament) *his holy Spirit*, to sanctifie *them*, as it sanctifieth him which is their head.

Thirdly, it is likewise confest; that what *Merit, Force, Vertue* or *Efficacie*, there is in the *sanctified body and blood* of Christ, we doe *freely, fully, and wholly* receiue it by *this Sacrament*.

Fourthly, all sides say, that the *effect* thereof *in vs*, is a *reall transmutation* of our Soules

A Preparation

from *sinne* to *righteousnesse*, from *Death* and corruption, to *Immortalitie* and Life.

Fiftly, all sides confesse, that because the Sacrament (I mean the *Bread* and *Wine*) being, of *it selfe*, but a corruptible and *earthly creature*, must needs be thought an *vnlikely instrument*, to worke so *admirable effects* in Man; we therefore are to *rest* our selues vpon *Gods Omnipotencie*, vpon the strength of his glorious and vnresistable power, who *is able* and *will* bring to passe, that the *Bread* and the *Cup* which he giueth vs, shal be *really* and *truely* that thing *which he promiseth*.

This is agreed on *all sides*, and *this is* as much as is *necessary* to be knowne and beleeued touching our *receiuing of Christ*, in the Sacrament, to the

the comfort of our Soules.

True it is, that by reason of *the neere coniunction* and *vnion* which is betwixt *Sacramentum & Rem Sacramenti*, betweene the outward *visible signes* of Bread and Wine, and the *inward inuisible grace*, the body and blood of Christ: the *ancient Fathers*, in their writings, doe call the Bread the Body; and the Cup, the Blood of Christ: because Sacraments vsually do beare the Names of the heauenly things, whereof they bee not empty, but exhibiting Signes. And as Doctor *Bilson* sheweth, because the people should regard, not the *Creatures* which they *saw*; but *chiefely* and *principally*, the *graces* which they *beleeue*. Therefore the *Fathers* euery where, without exception, doe call the

Ad Apolog. Ies. par.4.p.728.

elements

elements by the names of *the inward* and *heauenly vertues*, that are annexed to *them*, and *conferred with them*, by the *truth* of his *Word*, and *Power* of his *Spirit*.

Moreouer, whensoeuer the *Fathers* doe propose the *dignitie*, *propriety*, and *efficacie* of the Sacrament; they do not mean the *Creatures* (which our *eyes* and *tasts* doe better iudge of, then *their tongues* can vtter, or their *wits* can teach vs) but that *other diuine, life-giuing* and *soule-sauing part* of the Sacrament, which our *hearts* by *faith* doe take hold on, and doe possesse *more really* and effectually, than if it were *chammed* in our mouths, or buried in our *stomacks*; as *they* of the *Romish Church* doe grosely conceiue. Which *two obseruations*, if they be be well remembred, will easily beare off the *dint* of all those allegations out of the Fathers, which they seeme to glory and *triumph* in so much.

For either, in *alledging the Fathers*, they doe mistake *one part* for *another*, supposing *that* to be *corporall*, which *indeed* is *spirituall*: or else they vrge the *Name* (which the *signe* beareth for *similitude*) as earnestly to *all intents*, as it were the *very thing* it selfe: which is the cause why the Papists do *misconstrue* so many *Texts*, and stray so far from the *Truth* in the handling of the doctrine of the Sacrament.

περὶ τὸ ὀρθῶς διδάσκειν δεῖ πρῶτον ἐξετάζειν τὰ ὀνόματα. To teach rightly the nature of this Sacrament, wee must first search into the *Names* which are giuen to it.

S. Damascen.

it. The Names giuen vnto it in Scripture are principally three. It is called *the Communion of the body and blood of Chrift*. Secondly, it is called the *Supper of the Lord*. Thirdly, a Commemoration of Chrift.

1.Cor.10.16.

1.Cor.11.20.

A *Communion* it is called, in regard of a *three-fold vnion*: that is, firft, in refpect of the *neere vnion* and coniunction which is betwixt the *parts* of this Sacrament; betwixt the *outward vifible Elements* of Bread and Wine, and the *inward inuifible graces* the bodie and blood of Chrift.

Secondly, *in regard of* the *neere vnion* which is betwixt *Chrift*, & euery *worthy receiuer*.

Thirdly, in refpect of the *vnion and coniunction* that is betwixt *all faithfull Receiuers*, as they are *members* of Chrift

Christ his *mysticall bodie*.

First, the *union* that is betwixt the *internall* and *externall* parts of the Sacrament, is partly touched *before*; and it is *founded* and grounded vpon the *infallible promise* of Christ, in these words: *This is my body which is broken for you; This Cup is the New Testament in my blood.* For howsoeuer *these words* doe seeme to bee but a *bare Narration*; yet, *in truth*, they are *words* of most *comfortable promise*: for *Narratio boni nobis obventuri, promissio est.* The *Narration of good which shall befall vs, is a promise.* A promise *Euangelicall*: for so much doth the word *vobis* imply. It is broken *for you*: shed *for you* and for *many* And *thus* we are to conceiue them: (*viz.*) by this *Bread*, as by a certaine pledge

1 Cor. 11.24,25

Luke. 22.20.
Mar. 14.24.

pledge or pawne, I doe assure you that *this my body* shall bee deliuered to death for *your sakes*, to obtaine for you a pardon and full remission of all your sinnes. And, by *this wine*, as by a sure and *certaine testimonie* or Sacrament, do I acertaine *you* that I will offer vp *my blood* to God my Father, that *by it* I may *ratifie* and confirme the *Couenant of grace* whereof I am ordained the Mediator. That hauing *paid this price for you*, you may be atoned and reconciled to God, and bee iustified, and saued. This vnion betweene the *visible and inuisible things* in the Sacrament, is not a *spirituall*, but a *Sacramentall* vnion, and it is *founded* vpon those fore-named words of Christ. For *bread* as it is *bare bread* is not the Sacramentall body

Alsted. Theo. Catechet. cap. 16.

body of Chrift, but as *it is cloathed* and apparelled with *Chrift his promife*, after Confecration. That, then, is *one regard* why this Sacrament is called a *Communion*.

Secondly, it is called a *Communion* in refpect of the neere *vnion* which is betwixt *Chrift* and *vs* which doe worthily receiue him *in* and by this Sacrament. Which *vnion* is not *Sacramentall*, but *fpirituall*. By vertue of which *fpirituall vnion*, we and all *worthy Communicants*, doe become bone of Chrifts bone, and flefh of Chrifts flefh: by this, wee be one with Chrift, and *Chrift one with vs*, as our Communion-booke faith. For as *Leo* (fpeaking of thofe which doe partake of the firft Sacrament, the Sacrament *of Baptifme*) faith,

Ephef. 5. 30.

Serm. 4. de Paff. Domini.

Corpus

Corpus regenerati fit caro Crucifixi. The *body of him that is regenerate, is become the flesh of our crucified Sauiour.* So *Cyril* speaking of *this other Sacrament* of Christs body and blood, saith, That we must consider, that *Christ is in vs*, not onely χίσει or by *conformitie* of our *affections* to *his*; but also by a *Naturall* (that is by a true and *Reall*) *participation*. Euen as if a Man should take *wax* molten with fire, and mingle it with other *wax* that were melted, so that they seeme to become *one* and the same Lumpe, *Sic communicatione corporis & sanguinis Christi, Ipse in nobis manet & nos in ipso.* So, by communicating *of the body and blood of Christ, Christ abideth in vs,* and *we in* him. Thus saith S. *Cyril.* We being therefore *by this Sa-*
cramment

In Ioan lib. 10. cap. 13.

crament vnited to Christ *spiritually*, are made *partakers of his Death* and *Passion*, of *his obedience*, *righteousnesse*, and *all other* his merits and benefits, as *truely* and as *fully*, and if wee *in our owne persons*, had suffered *his paines*, performed the Law, and fulfilled *all Righteousnesse*, and *God* doth looke vpon *vs*, and regard *vs* with loue & compassion, as if *we were the very flesh and limbs of his owne deare Son*. And this is *a second regard*, in respect wherof this Sacrament is called *a Communion*.

Thirdly, it is called a *Communion*, in respect of the *Vnion* that is made betwixt *one and another*; betwixt *all beleeuers* among themselues: who, by this Sacrament, doe *professe* themselues to be not *only members* of Christ, but also *one anothers*

others *members*. Christ assuring vs, *thereby*, that wee are *very members of his mysticall body*, which is the *blessed company of all faithfull people*, as our common Prayer-booke saith. This is part of the *Communion of Saints*, which wee speake of in our Creed. So that this *vnion* is neither *sacramentall*, nor *spirituall*, but *Mysticall*: an vnion with the *mysticall members* of Chrifts mysticall Body, the *Corporation* or *company* of *Beleeuers*. For wee which are many are *one body*, and *one Bread*, because *wee all are partakers of one Bread*. By which wee are taught, that this is a Sacrament *of Loue and Charitie*. In consideration *whereof* it was called Ἀγάπη, *Charitie*: because the duty of Christian *loue* is required in *all* which are to communicate:

1.Cor.10.17.

to the Sacrament.

municate: of which grew their *Loue-feasts*, or feasts of *Charity* in the *Primitiue Church* at the celebration of the Lords Supper. Concerning which *Tertullian* discourseth at large; *Cœna nostra, de Nomine rationem sui ostendit: vocatur enim Agape, id quod Dilectio penes Grecos est, &c.*

Now this Christian *Charity*, which is especially to be exercised at the solemnizing of this Sacrament, doth shew forth it selfe principally in two things, *in condonando, & Donando*, in forgiuing, and giuing.

The *first*, is a *ready affection* to forgiue *iniuries* done vnto vs. Whereunto we should bee the *rather* induced, because the *party* whom we are to forgiue is our *Brother*, one of our *owne members*, and a *member of Iesus Christ:*

Iude verse 12.

In Apologetico aduersus gentes cap. 9.

Christ: Wee cannot hate, or smite, or wrong *him* againe; but wee must also hate, smite, and *wrong* our *Sauiour Christ*. *Saul, Saul, why persecutest thou me? saith our Sauiour* to *S. Paul*, who persecuted his *poore members* on earth. Christ takes the *wrong* or hurt that is done to *any* of *his members*, as done to himselfe. Therefore our Sauiour chargeth his *Disciples*, if a Brother doe offend them, *to forgiue him seuenty times seuen times*. And will haue *our gift* left before the *Altar* (that is, his owne *immediate worship omitted*) rather then the *Reconciliation* of our Brethren bee neglected. For whosoeuer shall come to *Gods board* with enuie or malice against his Brother or Sister, hee doth *most impiously mocke* and deride the *Lord* in silence;

Acts 9.

Math. 18. 22.

Math. 5. 24.

silence, making *as though hee* and his *Brother* were all *one*, most perfect friends, when by hatred, or malice, his heart is *most hostilly* diuided from him. Can we desire, or expect, from the *Lord*, pardon for *our offences*, as wee forgiue others, and not otherwise, and yet doe we retaine malice against our neighbour? *Good Christians* are to haue a speciall care of *that*, lest *God* serue them, as hee did the *vnmercifull seruant*, to whom hee had forgiuen *ten thousand Talents*, when God sees *him* take his *fellow* by the *throat*, for a *trifle* of a poore *hundred pence*, and cast him into prison; he *reuokes* his former promise of pardon, and deliuers him ouer to the *Iaylors*, till hee had paid the *vtmost farthing*. Mat.18.33,34. Our offences against God are

K 2 *Talents*,

Talents, heauy debts, yet in *this Sacrament* he seales a *pardon* of them; the *offences* of our *brethren* to vs can be but *as pence* in comparison of *Talents*: And *ours* against God, are *thousands*, yea, *ten thousands*; our *brothers* against *vs* are (at the most) but *hundreds*. So God suffers from vs an *hundred* iniuries, for *one* that wee suffer from our brother. Ours against God (being *Talents*) and our Brothers offences against vs (being but *pence*) doe exceed the wrongs which we can receiue from our neighbour as much as foure hundred pound doth in value surmount one Iewish peny.

The *second* thing in which *Charitie* consisteth, is in *Donando*, in giuing: Therefore as we professe *this vnion* with our *fellow-members*, so wee must

put

put on the *bowels of compassion*; and by that meanes, *make our selues* to feele in our soules *that* calamitie, and *those* euils which *they* suffer, and make *them* partakers of *those blessings* which we enioy.

And because Saint *Iohn* saith, if a man haue *the wealth of this world and see his brother want, how dwelleth the loue of God in him? My little Children let vs not loue in word onely, but in deed and in Truth. For if a Brother or a Sister be naked and destitute of dayly food; and you say, Depart in peace; warme your selues, and fill your bellies: notwithstanding you giue them not those things which are needfull for the body, what helpeth it?* Therefore *at Communions* it was euer in *vse* to haue *Collections* and *Oblations* for

1.Iohn 3.17.

Iam.2.15.16.

for the poore, in which regard the Greeke Fathers called this Sacrament ~~προσφορα~~, an *Oblation*. And our Church appointeth an *Offertorie* at the Communion, and *Almes* to bee gathered for the poore. For whatsoeuer is giuen to the *poore members* of Iesus Christ, is not *giuen*, but *lent*; and *lent* not *freely*, but vpon *vsury*; and not *common vsury* (as ten in the hundred) but on *encrease of a thousand* fold in this life, and *eternall happinesse* in the life to come.

From two of these *vnions* there resulteth a two-fold *presence* of the *body* and *blood* of Christ in this Sacrament. The *first* is in respect of the *Consecrated Elements of Bread and Wine*, to which the body and blood of Christ are *present sacramentally*. That is, as they are
signes,

signes, and haue a *Reference* and Relation to the things *signed and signified* by them; which *relation* dependeth vpon the *institution* and ordination of Christ. *This presence* doth consist in *this*, that *so often* as the *bread* and *wine* in the holy Sacrament, are *offered* to any Communicant; at the *same instant* the *body & blood* of *Christ*, doe also *present* themselues truely to the *Soule* of that person: as, in the *word*, Christ is truely offered to *those*, that *heare it*, and howbeit the *hallowed Bread and Wine* be neuer separated from *the things* which they doe *seale* and *signifie*, but doe *alwayes offer* them by vertue of that *promise*, which they doe *seale* and *confirme*: yet God, to *none* but *Beleeuers*, doth *inwardly* performe

A Preparation

forme that, which *outwardly* he *offereth.*

2 Therefore in the *second* place wee are to consider the *presence* of Christs body, which doth concerne the *Communicants* themselues ; to whose soules no doubt but it *is truely and really present*, if so bee *they doe beleeue* in the Sonne of the liuing God. The *Reall presence* of Christs most blessed *body and blood,* is *not* to be *sought* for therefore *in* the consecrated Bread and Wine, but *in* the worthy *receiuer* of them. And with this the *very order* of our *Saujours words* agreeth. First, *Take and eate* : Then, *This is my body which was broken for you* : First, *Drinke ye all of this* : Then followeth, *This is my blood of of the New Testament, which is shed for many, for the remission of*

Alsted, Sect. 2. c. 16

to the Sacrament.

of sinnes. I see not *which way* (saith that exact Diuine Master *Hooker*) it should be *gathered by the words of Christ, when,* and *where* the *Bread* is the *Body,* or the *Cup* the *blood,* but onely in the *very heart* and *soule* of him which receiueth *them.* And in *the soule* of man *whole Christ* is *more really* present, by faith, then it is (according to the *popish grosse conceit*) in the *formes* of bread and wine, as the *profound and Reuerend* B. *Bilson* teacheth at large. For, that the *substance of Bread* should bee turned into the *substance* of *Christ his body,* is a thing altogether *impossible,* by the confession of their *owne Cannon Law. Hoc tamen est Impossibile, quòd panis sit Corpus Christi.*

Secondly, this holy Sacrament, in Scripture, is called the *Supper*

De Consecrat. Distinct. secund. sect. panis est in Altari. Gloss. ibi.

A Preparation

Supper *of the Lord*: a *holy Feast*, a *spirituall banquet*, and it consisteth of βρῶσις καὶ πόσις, of meat and drinke. The *spirituall meat* which our *soules* are to feed vpon, is the *flesh of Christ*, (*represented* and *exhibited by the sacramentall bread*) and the *spirituall drinke* wherewith we are refreshed, is the *blood* of Christ (*signified and conueyed vnto vs by the consecrated wine in the Cup.*) So our Sauiour teacheth vs. *My flesh is meat in deed and in truth* : (ἀληθῶς) *and my blood is drinke indeed* ; not in shew, and appearance onely, but in *good earnest* and *truth*. And as in *this* Supper *both* the body and blood of Christ be *offered* vnto vs, for our *ghostly refection*: So also *both* the one, and the other are *verily* and *indeed taken* and receiued of the faithfull in the Lords

1.Cor.11.20.

Iohn 6.55.

Lords Supper; as *our Church teacheth in the Catechisme*.

Man consisteth of two *parts*; of a *body* and a *Soule*. A *sensitiue* body which hee hath *common* with *bruite* creatures; and an *vnderstanding* soule, or Spirit, wherein hee *resembleth* the Cœlestiall *Angels*: and *both* these parts doe require a kinde of *food proper* to preserue their *seuerall* liues. That, as by *bodily food, vita animalis*, the naturall and sensitiue life is preserued in *being*: so by *some* food, or Diet, *conuenient* for the soule and spirit, *it* may be preserued to an *immortall* and *supernaturall* life.

It is able to *strike* a man into an *astonishment*, if hee doe but *seriously* meditate on the *wonderfull* prouidence and riches of *Almighty God*, in that hee prouideth bodily *food* and *sustenance* for *euery* liuing creature. For the *innumerable Hosts* and Armies of *Birds, Beasts, Fishes* and *creeping things*, that are in all the world. *We see* what a *mighty* trouble and charge it is to vittaile a *Nauy* consisting but of an *hundred sayle* for a *few* moneths; what *great* prouision is made to maintain them *at Sea*: which ships may containe *perhaps* forty or *fifty thousand* men. But what are *fifty* or an *hundred* thousand, to those *innumerable thousands* which liue vpon the face of the *whole* earth? And *yet* God prouideth *meat* for *euery one of them*. And not for *Men* onely, but for *euery other* liuing creature, according to it *seuerall* kinde, and that not for a *few moneths*, but for *many yeares*, euen *during* the

to the Sacrament.

the continuance and lasting of their liues. And *such meat* too, as is *agreeable* to their seuerall *appetites*. He giueth them *their* meat: Meat *proper* to their seuerall stomacks: and not *so onely*; but he giues it them *then*, when it is most *seasonable* for them to eate it. He giueth their meat in *due season*, saith the Psalmist. and all this without any *trouble*, or *paines-taking*. What a *rich*, *wise*, *prouident* King is the Lord?

Psal.145.15.

But whereas to *all other* liuing creatures he hath assigned *one* onely kind of *meat* (to some *grasse*; to some, *corne*; to some, *flesh onely*, &c.) and for *drinke* hath appointed them all nothing but *water*: yet to *man* he giueth *variety* of *dainties*, (*Fish*, and *Flesh*, and *Foule*; *Hearbs*, *Spices*, and *Fruits*.) And for his
drinke

A Preparation

drinke hee hath giuen him not onely *water*, but *variety* of liquors of delicatest relishes, and the *iuice* & *blood* of Grapes and other fruits. Hath God *so liberally* and plentifully prouided for the sustenance of these *mortall bodies* of ours? and hath he not as *great* care of our *better part*, our soule? hath he not prouided *meat* for *it*, to preserue and maintaine *it* in a *spirituall*, and to an *immortall life?*

Yes, surely, in *this Supper* he doth feed vs to *immortall life*. And the *dainties* which he sets before our *soules* to feed vpon, doe *surpasse all other* bodily food, by many degrees. For here are *Dapes Dapsiles, Dapes Regiæ, Abundance of dainty dishes, Banquets Royall, food for Kings.* Nay, in *this Supper*, there are set before vs not onely
Dapes

to the Sacrament.

Dapes Regiæ, meat for Kings: but *the very flesh and body of the King* of all *Kings*.

But you may say, *here* being but *one* onely *kinde of meat* in this Supper and banquet of the Lord; how can it bee counted such a *sumptuous* and *Princely* Feast?

I answer: It is like vnto *Manna*, wherewith the *Lord* fed the children of *Israel* in the wildernesse. This *Manna*, being but *one kinde of meat*, had *in it* abundance and all variety of *pleasant tasts*, and dainty relishes. It was meet for *all tastes; Sapiebat cuique prout voluit*. Look what pleasant taste a man did desire, that it should haue in his mouth, the *same it tasted like*. Therefore our *Sauiour* compares his *flesh* to Manna, and prefers it before *Manna*.

Wisd. 16.

Iohn 6.49.58.

Mul-

Multitude and varietie of diuers things, which doe all serue but *to one and the same end* and purpose, doth argue *some want* and imperfection in *euery* of those things in *seuerall*. Therefore it is *Natures custome, Multiplicare res imperfectas*, to multiply such things as are *imperfect*; so we see that there bee a *huge multitude* of *Starres*, helping *one another* to giue light to the darknes of the *night*; when as there is but *one* onely *Sunne*, to illuminate the *day*. Wherefore, seeing that no *one good* thing *created* by God; (no, nor *all of them* ioyned together,) could *fill* the vast appetite of *mans soule*, or satisfie the *stomack or desire thereof* to the *full*. The wisedome of God, in *this Supper*, hath prepared for vs, such an *admirable, complete,*
and

and *perfect* dish, that *if by faith we doe truely eate of it, we shall not hunger for euer.*

Iohn 6.35.

But it may bee asked, why Christ, promising vs *food* and diet for our *soules*, should giue vs his *Flesh?* How can the *soule*, being a substance *spirituall*, bee fed with *Flesh*, which is a *bodily* substance? And, if it be his purpose to *free* vs from *corruption* (whereunto the *eating of the forbidden fruit* had made vs obnoxious,) if his *minde* were to *restore* and raise vs vp to *Immortality*; why doth hee prescribe vs *Flesh*, for our *Diet?* especially, considering that *Flesh*, *of it selfe*, is *mortall* and subiect to corruption and *dissolution?*

This doubt may be easily remoued, if we consider the *words* of *Christ* narrowly. For hee doth

doth not *simply* affirme, that *flesh* (in generall) is meat for the Soule; but *Caro Mea, My flesh*, saith Christ, is *meat indeed*. For Flesh; of *it selfe*, cannot be food for the *soule*; because flesh is subiect to *corruption*, and *profiteth nothing*. But if it bee *Caro Mea*, Christ *his flesh*; if flesh be vnited to a *person* in the Deitie (as *Christ his flesh* was) it can free vs from *mortality* and corruption, and conueigh vnto vs the *life* of *eternitie*.

Iohn 6.65.

What and if we *adde* (as we *may* and *must* most truely) that the *meat* which Christ giueth vnto vs at this *heauenly* banket, is not his body *onely*, but his *soule* also? nay, his *whole person*: namely, the *essentiall word* of God in *which* both *his body* and *soule* doe subsist, and to *which* they are *personally* & *inseparably* vnited. Now

Now where the *person* of the *Sonne* is, there is *also* the whole *Deitie*; and where the *Deity* is, there are all the *three persons* of the *Trinitie*. Therefore by this *Meat* (howbeit after a *diuerse manner*) the *body* and *soule* of Christ, his *Diuine* and *Humane* Nature, and the *whole Trinity* of persons is conueyed vnto vs. Therefore (deare Christian) consider wel with thy selfe, how much thou art indebted to *Christ* thy *Sauiour*; who in *this Supper* doth giue vnto thee *that* which in *value*, *price* and *dignity* doth far surmount the *whole world*, and *all creatures* that are contained in the compasse thereof.

Wherefore that our *soule* cannot be aduanced to *Immortality* by eating *flesh*, it is most certaine: if so bee that Christ had meant *that* flesh whereof the Prophet *Esay* spake, when hee saith, *omnis Caro fœnum,* All flesh is grasse. But of *this flesh,* which is vnited to the *eternall Word* of *God*, it is *not* true. For, *si verbum caro factum sit,* if *that word bee made flesh,* it will communicate *life, Immortalitie,* and *freedome from corruption* to *this* flesh, as *Dauid* teacheth. *Thou wilt not suffer thine holy One to see corruption.*

Esay 40.6.

Iohn 1.14.

Psal. 16.

Hence it is that our Sauiour doth cal *his Flesh, liuing Bread:* because it is so, both *formaliter, in se;* and *Effectiuè, in nobis:* because it hath life *formally in it selfe ;* and also doth *giue life,* by it's *vertue* and *operation,* in *vs,* who do partake of it. So *Christ* speaketh; *I am the liuing bread, which came downe from Heauen.*

Iohn 6. 51.

If

If any Man eate of *this bread*, he shall *liue for euer*. And the *bread* which I will giue is *my flesh*, which I will giue for the *life* of the world.

But, though I am but *dust* and *ashes*, yet let not *my Lord* be *angry* if I aske him *one question*: How can it be, that thy *flesh* should become *meat*; or thy *bloud* be made *drinke*? Art not thou *God*? The *God* that giuest *food* to *all* flesh? And will not *Hereticks* and carnall men *dis esteeme* thy *Maiestie*, when they shal heare that thou maist be eaten and drunken, as meat and drinke? will they not thinke that thou art *not God*? Remember, I pray thee, the deuice and cunning that *Moses* vsed among the Israelits, when hee went about to perswade them, that the golden Calfe

(which

(which *they* adored as a *God*) was no *God* at *all*, but a vaine and empty *Idol*. He breakes the Calfe in pieces, grinds it to powder, and giues it to the Israelites to drinke off. As if hee should haue said; Consider O *ye vnwise* among the people, O *yee fooles* when will yee vnderstand? Can that *Puppet* and *Idol* which yee haue eate and drunke, and swallowed downe into your bellies bee any *True God*? Forsake your Errour therefore, and consider that *this Calfe* which you haue drunke and swallowed, cannot be God. Which being *so*, how canst *thou* (Lord Iesus!) who art the euerliuing God become *meat* and *drinke* to vs? will not *Infidels* and *Heretiques* take occasion *from hence* to cauill, and say, that thou art not *Consubstantiall*

stantiall with thy Father, and (consequently) that *thou* art *not God?*

But the *answer* is very easie, if wee take notice of the *difference* which is betwixt *liuing* meat, and *that* which is *dead*. Meat, which is *slaine* and *dead*, before we feed on it, is by *concoction* conuerted and changed, from it *owne* substance, into the *substance of our bodies*; *as, per nos, viuit in Nobis*, and doth *liue* in vs, by meanes of *our owne* life, after digestion. And of such kinde was the *golden Calfe* which *Moses* gaue the *Israelites* to swallow down. And therefore his *Argument* was strong and firme, that the *golden Calfe* was no *God*, because the Israelites did take it into their stomacks; by the naturall *heat whereof* it was altered and

and *turned* into *their* flesh and blood. All which things are repugnant, and contrary to the *Nature of God*, which is *immutable* & incapable of *change* & *alteration*; as himself proclaimes by *Malachy*. *Ego Dominus, & nõ mutor*, I am the Lord, I change not. But if the meat that we feed vpon be *liuing* meat; Then the *case is altered*: for *liuing* meat will *alter* and *change thee*, who doest feed on it, into the Nature, or *quality* of *it selfe*.

Therefore *this heauenly* food (seeing that it containeth the *Author of Life*, in it) *we*, when we eate it, doe not transmute and *turne it* into our substance, but *it* (being eaten) doth spiritually *transforme* and conuert *vs* into the substance of *it selfe*: as Saint *Augustine* bringeth *it* in speaking to *himselfe*. *Non tu me*

Mal.3.6.

me mutabis in te, sed tu mutaberis in me; Thou shalt not change me into thy self, but thou shalt be *changed & transmuted* into me. Wherefore Saint *Paul*, who had fed liberally and frequently on *this* food, doth professe that he found this strange alteration in himselfe. *Viuo ego, jam non ego, sed viuit in me Christus.* I *liue*, yet *not I now*, but *Christ* liueth in *me*. And our Sauiour intimates no lesse, when hee saith, Hee that *eateth* my flesh, and *drinketh* my blood, *dwelleth* in *me*, and I in *him*.

But *without drinke* the banquet is no banquet, the feast is no feast: Therefore in this supper our Sauiour setteth before vs not onely βρῶσιν, but πίσιν. not onely *meat*, but *drink* also. And the *drinke* here, which he offereth vnto vs, is his *owne* most
pre-

Gal.2.10.

Iohn 6.56.

precious *blood*. [*My blood is drinke indeed*]

True it is, that in the *old law*, *blood* of Sacrifices might neither bee *eaten* nor drunke. And that, either for *reuerence sake*, because it was a type of the blood of *Christ*, who was to be sacrificed for *vs*: or, because it was a Token and Argument of a cruell and bloody disposition: or, because the *life* of the flesh was *in* the Blood: or, because *blood* was appointed to be *offered* to God vpon the *Altar*, as an *oblation* to make *legall* expiation for sinnes, *Leuit*. 17. as if God had said; I will not permit you to taste of the Blood of your Sacrifices, because it is reserued to be offered vpon mine Altar for sinne. But Christ, speaking of *his blood*, saith, *Bibite ex hoc omnes*, Drinke ye all of *this*. Where-

Cyprian Serm. de Cœna Dom. Noua est huius Sacramenti doctrina, & Doctore Christo primùm hæc mundo innotuit Disciplina, vt biberent Sanguinem, cuius esum legis Antiquæ authoritas districtissimè interdicit. Lex prohibet esum Sanguinis; Evangeliū præcipit, vt bibatur.

to the Sacrament.

Wherein there appeareth *in* the *blood* of Christ a twofold excellency, beyond *all* other *blood* that was offered to God in sacrifice. One of *these, some* will haue to be signified by the Psalmist, *Psal.* 51.7. *Asperges me Domine Hyssopo, & mundabor; lavabis me, & super nivem dealbabor.* Thou shalt *sprinkle* mee with Hyssope, and I shall bee *cleane*; thou shalt *wash* me, and I shall be *whiter* then the *Snow*. Where we are to *note* the difference betweene *aspergere* and *lavare*, betwixt *sprinkling* and *washing*.

For, to *sprinkle*, a *few drops* of water are sufficient: but, to *wash* (especially if the spot or stain be *sunke deepe* in) *good store* of water is required. Such is the difference, betwixt the blood of Christ, & the blood of the *legall sacri-*

sacrifices. The blood of the *Mosaicall* sacrifices, being offered to God, did wipe away certain *irregularities* and *ceremoniall impurities*; and the maine *vertue of them* consisted *therein*, because it did but onely *aspergere*, *besprinkle:* but Christ his blood doth *wash* and *rinse*, and purge the *soule* from *all kinds* of sins and wickednesse. So wee are taught by *Iohn the Diuine, Apocal.* 1.5. He *hath washed* vs from our finnes *in his blood.* As if *Dauid* had sayd, If thou *besprinkle* mee with the blood of *lambes* or *birds*, I grant indeed that I shall be *cleane* from some *externall impurities* and *irregularities:* but if thou *wash* mee with the *blood* of *Christ*, then I shall be *whiter* then the *snow*.

A *second* excellency of *this* Blood aboue *all other*, may appeare peate by *this*: namely, that God iudging the dignity and *price* of the *blood* of legall sacrifices to be but *poore* and *meane*, would not suffer that blood to be vsed as *meat and drinke*, and to serue *for sacrifice* also. Therefore the Lord saith, I *haue giuen* it (not *to be eaten & drunk*) but to *offer* vpon the *Altar*, for to make an *atonement* for your soules. That is, I gaue it, to the end you should *offer* it to Mee; not that you should *eate and drink* of it your selues. But *Christ* his *blood* is of such an *infinite* price and excellency, that it wil serue for *both*: viz. not onely to *refresh* our thirsty soules, as *drinke* doth the body; (for, *my blood* saith he, *is drinke indeed*) but also an *oblation* and *sacrifice* to clense vs from sinnes: as St. *Iohn* saith, The *blood* of Iesus Christ

Leuit. 17. 11.

A Preparation

1 Iohn 1.7.

Christ *clenseth* vs from *all sinne*. And, *He* is the *propitiation* for our sinnes, and not for *ours onely*, but for the sins of the *whole world*. So that Christ hath *blood* enough, and *that* of *vertue* enough, both to *satisfie* for our *sinnes*, and also to *feed* vs to *eternall life*.

1 Iohn 2.2.

This blood which wee taste of in this *heauenly* banquet, it is of *most diuine* efficacy and vertue. For, but by God, no such effects can be produced. For *this blood* is that wherewith our *sins are taken away*. *Effunditur in remissionem peccatorum.* And that is *Casus Deo reseruatus*, a thing *peculiar & proper* to God alone [*To forgiue sinnes by his owne authority*.] Besides, it serueth not onely to *clense* our soules from *sinnes*, 1 Iohn 1.7. but it is wondrous good for

Mat. 26.

medicine

medicine also, and will heale the vlcers, and cure the wounds of our galled consciences. For *Ejus livore sanati sumus*, By his stripes *we* are *healed*. In which regard, it is *not vnlike* the blood of the Pellican, as *Dauid* compareth *Christ*, when hee brings him *in*, saying, *Similis factus sum Pellicano*, I became like a Pellican. Saint *Hierome* writing vpon those words, sayth; When the *Pellican* beholdeth her *young* ones brought almost to *death* by the sting of a *Serpent*, she digges an *hole* in her brest with her beake, and *from thence* fetcheth out blood; which lighting vpon and besprinkling *them*, *doth kill* the poyson of the Serpents sting, and restore them to life: But *Christ*, not contented to haue his *brest*, his *head*, his *sides*, his *hands*,

Esay 53.5.
1 Pet. 2. 24.

Psal. 102.

hands and *feet* pierced and opened, that he might *besprinkle vs with his blood, and so reuiue vs* that were *dead* in trespasses, and sinnes, by the *poysonous sting* of the old Serpent, doth in this Sacrament, communicate *all of it* to vs *mystically*: that by it (as by a most precious Balme) we might bee kept and preserued from *sinnes to come. Vt pretioso sanguinis illius Balsamo, nostris medeatur vulneribus*, saith holy *Bernard*.

Moreouer, *by it* there is *peace* and reconciliation made betwixt *God* and *vs*: and therefore it is called *Sanguis fœderis*, the blood of the League and *Couenant* betwixt *God* and *man*. Whereby God *bindeth* himselfe to become our *friend*, and receiue vs to grace and fauour, and *we* in like manner (on

Apoc. 12. 9.

our

our parts) do *bind* our selues to doe him *homage* and *fealty*: that is, keepe his lawes, and not to giue any *consent* to rebell against *him*.

There was among *diuers Nations* (at the making of Leagues of sincere loue & perfect friendship) a quaint ceremony in vse, and that was, to *mingle their bloods* together; and, so, to drinke them. The *Scythians* in all their *Couenants* of Friendship, vsed to carouse cups full of *blood* one to another. The *Arabians* with sharpe *Flint-stones* cut their skinnes, and opened their veynes to let out their *blood*: the *Garamantes* in *Lybia* drank and suckt blood off, mutually: The *Medes* and *Lydians* lanced their shoulders, and did eate and drinke the blood which issued frō thence, to confirme *peace* & friendship betwixt them, and the reason hereof (as some groūd their cōiecture) was, because, the *life being seated in the blood*, they wold signifie *hereby*, that *they* would rather *shed their bloods*, & lose their *liues*, then they would violate the *vow* and *Couenant* betwixt them made. *So* Christ (to shew that *this couenāt & league* of loue and friendship betwixt *him* and *vs*, doth remaine *firme* and *sure*) doth giue vs his most precious *blood* to drinke.

If it bee demanded, why Christ doth giue vs *his* blood alone, or, why he doth not require *vs*, to open a *veine*, and mix *our blood* with *his*, and so drinke it off? or, why for the *confirmation* of *this* couenant he doth not drink our *blood* too?

It may be answered, that, the
reason

reason was; because, to the end that *God* should be made *Man*, it was not *necessary* that *he* should drinke mans blood: but, to the end that *Man* (as S. *Peter* saith) *might bee made partaker of the diuine Nature*, it was necessary that *he* should *drink* the blood of *God*. Therefore our Sauiour saith, *Except ye drink* his blood, *yee haue* no life *in you*.

2. Pet. 1.4.

Iohn 6.54.

If we drinke *his* blood; then, (*it* being, and *remaining in vs*, and hee being of the *blood Royall*) we may *boldly* say, that wee haue of the *Blood Royoll* within vs. And by *that blood* we haue *Title* to a *Crowne*, to a *Kingdome*; to a *Crowne* of *Glory*, to the *Kingdome* of Heauen. And *by this* we may assure our selues that wee are the *sonnes of God*: because we haue *in vs* the very *flesh* and *blood* of his *onely begotten*

ten Sonne: we, by this meanes (viz. by *eating* and *drinking him*) are become *bone* of *his bone*, and *flesh* of *his flesh*.

Ephes.5.30.

For as of *meat*, drink, & of the *party* that feedeth vpon them, *one substance* is made *naturally*: so of this *diuine meat & drinke*, and of vs, that eate and drink it, is made *one substance spiritually*; and so our Communion Book teacheth, saying; *Then we dwell in Christ, & Christ dwels in vs: Then, we be* one *with Christ, & Christ with vs*. And, if by the *blood* of the *Paschal Lambe* sprinkled vpon the doore-posts of the Israelites in Egypt, the *destroying Angell* was kept and restrained from *hurting any* of the Israelites, (whereas he slew all the *first-borne* thorow the *whole kingdom* of *Egypt*:) *much more* shall the *blood* of Iesus Christ

Christ (not *sprinkled* onely vpon our *hearts*) but *thorowly digested* in our soules and consciences, preserue our *bodies and soules* from eternal destruction?

Very *glorious things* are spoken of *thee*, O thou *blood* of *God*! For Saint *Chrysostome* among many *glorious things* which he speaketh of *thee*, doth tell me, that *Dæmones, cùm Dominicum sanguinem in nobis vident, in Fugam vertuntur*; *The very Deuils, when they see the blood of the Lord* in vs, are turned backe and *put to flight*.

But very *abominable things* are *done* to *thee*, O thou *blood* of *God*! For *now adayes*, men (in stead of *receiuing* thee into *their soules*, by faith, to *sanctifie* their *hearts* and minds) they doe receiue thee into *their mouths* onely, to put *them into swearing*

Chrysost. hom. 45 super Ioan. cap. 6.

ring (by the blood of God, by the *blood of Christ*, is too frequent in the mouths of the *most*) but *Lord* giue them *grace* to *value* thy blood, and *Lord* forgiue their blasphemies. For *thy blood speaketh better things then the blood of Abel.* His blood cryed for *vengeance*; thine did and doth cry for *pardon* and forgiuenesse; euen for *those* who did shed *it*, & blaspheme *thine honour*.

Heb.12.24.

But whatsoeuer hath beene said (as *who can say enough?*) of the blood of Christ, I would haue to be *rightly* conceiued: That I meane it of the *Sacrament*, so *farre* as it is *entire*, and not *diuided*: that is, as it consisteth not onely of an *outward visible* signe, but *also* of an *inward inuisible grace*; without which inward inuisible grace, the

the *outward signe*, being receiued, doth not *profit*, but rather *hurt*, and that very much, as we may read, 1. *Cor.* 11.29. διπλοῦν ἢ τὸ αἷμα τοῦ κυρίου. Τὸ μὲν γὰρ ἐστὶν αὐτοῦ σαρκικὸν ᾧ τ᾽ φθορᾶς λελυτρώμεθα τὸ δὲ πνευματικὸν, τουτέστιν ᾧ κεχρίσμεθα. Καὶ τοῦτ᾽ ἐστι πιεῖν τὸ αἷμα τοῦ Ἰησοῦ, τῆς κυριακῆς μεταλαβεῖν ἀφθαρσίας. There is a *twofold blood* of Christ: The *one* is bodily, that blood which was *in his flesh*; *whereby* we are freed and *ransomed* from perdition and corruption. The *other* is *spirituall, that* is it, by which we are *anointed*. And *this* is to *drinke* the *blood* of Iesus; *to wit*, to bee partakers of the Lords *incorruption* and *immortality*.

Seeing then as it hath beene said, this *blessed Sacrament* is a Supper and heauenly Banquet, let vs *try* our selues whether we we *come* to it with so good *affections*, as we would come to a bodily Supper, to a great mans Table.

First, we are to see whether there be in vs that which euery man will afford; that is inuited to the Table of some mighty Potentate; namely, *thankes* for the *message* to him that bid vs; whether we *accept*, or *refuse it*; which doth teach vs to powre forth *most hearty thankes* that we are vouchsafed to be called and inuited by the *God of heauen and earth* to this *heauenly banquet*. The second is, that which our Sauiour deliuered *by precept*: That is, to take the *lowest roome* at Feasts. Whereby we are taught, that, cōming to this *heauenly banquet*, euery man must in his own heart and *estimation*, set himselfe *low*, and become

Luke 14. 10.

become *vile* in his owne eyes. Wee must confesse our selues *vnworthy so much as to gather vp the crummes vnder the Lords Table*. And we must be so farre from contemning *any other* person that commeth and is *noted* for a *sinner*, that *wee* are to acknowledge *our selues* to bee not only *haynous* sinners, (as indeed we are, euen the *holiest* of vs all) but that we are the very *chiefe* of all *sinners*, as S. *Paul* doth.

<small>Com. Booke.</small>

<small>1 Tim.1.15.</small>

And this is a *third thing*, which commonly is in *such* as are bidden to great feasts, viz. to come with *affection*, with *appetite*, and *desire* to the *meat*, that is set before them. If it be a *vanity* to eate when there is *no hūger*; to drink for *cōpany*, when there is no *thirst*; then surely it is *very dangerous* to come to this

this *Feast* without *hunger* and *thirst* after Iesus Christ.

And as it is a discredit to *him* that hath prepared a *Supper*, to see his *guests* refuse to *come*, so *much more* griefe is it to see thē sit as if they had left their *stomackes* behind them at *home*.

Therefore, in the *feare of God*, let euery one stir vp himselfe and consider what *excellent diet* is set before vs, and by all meanes possible let vs *prouoke* our appetite and *desire* vnto it. For what a griefe was it to *Esau* to bring his *sauoury* meat, when his father had *no stomacke*? And what a *subtill counsell* was that of *Rebecca* to preuent *Esau*, and whilst the *old man* was *hungry*, to bring such *meat* as he liked? and the meat being *so liked*, caused *Isaac* to blesse *Iacob*. So this presēt meat when

to the Sacrament.

when it is liked & *longed for* of vs, it makes our soules to bleſs & *praiſe* God for the *ſame*, & *him* (conſequently) to *bleſſe* vs.

But it hath pleaſed the *Church of Rome* to *rob* and depriue the *lay-people* of the benefit of the *one part* of this Sacrament; and *that too,* directly *contrary* to the inſtitution and *ordinance* of our bleſſed Sauiour; who in *expreſſe* tearmes ſaith, *Bibite ex hoc OMNES,* Drinke yee ALL of *this*. — Mat.26.27. Marke 14. Luke 22.

It is *contrary* alſo to the *doctrine* of the *Apoſtle*, cleane thorow the latter part of the 11 *Chapter* of the *firſt Epiſtle* to the *Corinthians*: who enioyneth the *participation* of the Body and Blood both: The *Cup* as well as the *Bread*, at the leaſt *foure times* in that paſſage: and he giues charge (not to the
Mini-

Ministers onely, or to the *Priests* of *Corinth*, but) to the whole *body of the Church*, that *then* liued at *Corinth*, euen to euery *lay-person worthily* to eate the *bread & body*; *worthily* to drink the *cup* and *blood* of the Lord. 1 *Cor.* 11. 27, 28, 29.

And as I said before, the *charge* is giuen to euery *man*, whether *Church-man* or *Layman*; *First*, to *examine* himself; and *then* (hauing performed *that duty* of examination) to eate of that *bread* and *drinke* of that *cup*; to receiue *both* the *parts* of the Sacrament. I maruell then why *lay-persons* shold be restrained from tasting the *Lords cup*, vnlesse it be that *his Holinesse* & his *creatures* would perswade the world that *Lay-persons* were not so much as ἄνθρωποι *Homines*, not reasonable

to the Sacrament.

ble *men*, but to bee numbred *inter pecora campi*, amongst the beasts of the field; *inter equos & mulos*, amongst *horses and mules which haue no reason nor vnderstanding*: and therefore they would haue *this sentence* restrained only to *their Priests*.

It was the *precept* of Christ, and the *practice* of the whole Church of God, to receiue this Sacrament, *not* vnder *one kind alone* (as of *Bread*) but vnder *both* kinds of *bread* and *wine*.

Saint *Chrysostome* (*in* 2 *Cor*. 8 *Hom*. 8.) saith; *Ea, quæ sunt Eucharistiæ, communia sunt omnia inter sacerdotem & populum*; *Such things as belong to* the Sacrament of *the Eucharist*, are *All* common *both* to the Priest and *people*.

And what saith old *Clemens Alexandrinus*? Ἡ δ᾽ ἀμφοῖν αὖθις κρᾶσις

So we may read in Jrenæus *lib* 4 *cap*. 14. *Justin Martyr Apologid* 2. *Basilius Magnus in Sermon de Baptism. Cyprian. ad Cornelium, Epist*. 2. *Hieronim. in Sophonia, cap*. 3. *Prosper. in sententiis, &c*.

κρᾶσις, ποτοῦ κὶ λόγε, ἐυχαειϲία κέκληται. The mixture of *both* in one, (namely, of the Hallowed *drinke* and *word*) is called the Eucharist: *whereof such as doe participate by faith,* ἀγιάζον] κὶ σῶμα, κὶ ψυχὴν, *are sanctified both in soule and body, Clement. Alex. Padag. lib. 2. cap. 2.* The *wine* then is *part* of the Eucharist as well as the consecrated *bread*: and if *it* be a *part* of it, *then* the *people* haue interest in the *cup*, as well as the *priests*; or else *Chrysostome* was farre mistaken.

Sure it was *so thought* in *after* times also: for *Charles* the *Great* was a mighty Prince; yet was he no *Priest*, but a *lay-person*: and yet hee said, *Sanguis Christi, qui à nobis in Sacramento sumitur, pro nobis effusus est in remissionem peccatorum*. The blood

blood of *Christ which is received by vs* (putting *himselfe* into the number) *in the Sacrament, was shed for vs for the remission of sinnes.*

If we descend *lower*, many hundred yeares, euen to the dayes of *Peter Lumbard*, wee shall see that *then* the *cup* of the Lord was *not* kept *backe* from the *people*. For *Lumbard* tels vs of no such thing: only he moues this question, viz. *Seeing that the body of Christ, being aliue, cannot be without blood, wherefore did he ordaine his body to bee eaten vnder the form of bread, and his blood to be drunke vnder the forme of wine?*

And for answer hereunto, *Hee doth not tell vs* of *halfe* Communions, vnder *one kind* (for *this robbery* and sacriledge was *yet vnknown* to the Church in

Carol. Magnus de Imaginib. lib. 3. cap. 6.

in *Lumbards* time) but hee *seekes about* for *other* answers to assoyle the doubt. And, saith he, That *Christ* might declare that he did assume *the whole nature* of man, to redeeme it *wholly* (both *body* and *soule*) therefore hee instituted this Sacrament to bee celebrated *vnder both kinds* of Bread and Wine, (the *bread* hauing relation to his *body* or *flesh*, and the *wine* to his *soule*, which is *seated* in the *Blood*) to signifie in *Christ* the susception and *assuming both* of soule and flesh, and the redemption & *deliuerance* of *both soule* and *flesh* in vs. And he alleageth the testimony of S.* *Ambrose*, who was *many hundred*

*Valet ad tuitionem Corporis & Animæ, quod percipimus: quia Caro Christi pro salute Corporis, Sanguis verò pro Animâ nostrâ offertur; sicut præfigurauit Moses: Caro, inquit, pro Corpore vestro offertur, Sanguis pro Animâ. Sed tamen sub vtrâque specie sumitur, quod ad vtrumq; valet: quia sub vtrâque sumitur ipse totus Christus. Sed si in altera tantùm sumeretur, ad alterius tantùm, id est, Animæ vel Corporis, non vtriusque pariter tuitionem valere significaretur. Ambros. in 1 Cor. 11.

yea res

yeares before *Lumbard*, and moueth the same question, and answereth to it in this manner: That *which wee doe receiue is of power to defend both our body and soule. Because the flesh of Christ is offered for the health and saluation* of our body, *and His blood* for our soules, as *Moses prefigured, &c.*

Againe; let it bee granted that we doe, vnder *either kinde*, receiue *whole Christ*, with all his benefits: yet, saith that *holy Father*, if it should be receiued in *one kinde* alone; it should signifie that it were powerfull to defend but *one onely part* of man (viz. either the *soule* or the *body*) and not *both* of them together. And it may bee that the *Worthies of our Church* had some relation to *those reasons* of Saint *Ambrose*, or *some such like*,

like, in *that* prayer which goeth *immediately* before Consecration in our *Communion Booke*; where we pray: *Grant vs therefore gracious Lord, so to eate the flesh of thy deare Sonne Iesus Christ*, and *to drinke his blood*, that our sinfull bodies *may bee made cleane* by his bodie, *and* our soules *washed thorow his most* precious blood. But, *howsoeuer*, certain it is that *Gelasius* the *Pope* (and you know, that they of the *Romish Church* doe maintaine that *the Pope cannot erre*:) doth stand vpon Record in their owne *Cannon Law* to haue condemned this *robbing* of the *Lords Cup* from Lay-people, for no *smaller offence* then *sacriledge*. His words be these: *Comperimus, quòd* quidam *sumptâ* tantummodò *Corporis Sacri portione,*

to the Sacrament.

ne, à Calice *Sacrati Cruoris abstineant : qui proculdubio (quoniam nescio quâ superstitione docentur astringi) aut* Integra Sacramenta percipiant, aut ab Integris *arceantur : quia* Diuisio vnius Eiusdemque *mysterij, sine grandi* Sacrilegio *non potest prouenire.*

Wee vnderstand that *some,* receiuing onely the *portion* of Chrifts *body,* doe abstaine from the *Cup of* his *Sacred blood :* which men (because vndoubtedly they are trained vp in I know not what *kinde of superstition,*) let them bee *constrained* either to receiue the *Sacrament whole,* or to be kept backe from *the whole :* Because this *diuiding* of *one* and the *same* Mysterie cannot bee without great *Sacriledge.* And *Chrysostome* is flat against this mutilation

Gelasius, de Consecrat. cap. Comperimus Distinct. 2.

Nec Superfluè sumitur sub vtraque specie : nam species panis ad carnem, & species vini ad animam refertur, cum vnum sit Sacramentum sanguinis, in quo sedes est animæ. Iamq̃ sumite sub vtraq, specie, vt significetur, quòd vtrumq, Christus assumpsit, carnem & animam : & quòd tàm animæ quàm corpori participatio valeat. Vnde, si sub vnâ tantum specie sumeretur, ad Tuitionem alterius non valere significaretur. Glossa. ibid.

lation & dismembring of this holy Sacrament, when hee teacheth thus: Καὶ ὁ καθάπερ ἐπὶ τῆς παλαιᾶς, τὰ μ̄ ὁ ἱερεὺς ἤσθε, τὰ δ̄ ὁ ἐρχόμν̄Θ, ᾗ ὁ θέμις ἦν τῷ λαῷ μετέχειν, ὧν μετεῖχεν ὁ ἱερεὺς, ἀλλὰ νῦν πᾶσιν ἓν σῶμα προσκεῖται, ᾗ ποτήριον ἕν. *It is not now*, as it was in the time of the *Old Testament*. When as the *Priest* did eate of *one part*, and the *people* another part (for it was *not lawfull* for the *people* to participate of those things, whereof the *Priest* did eate:) but *now* (to wit, in the time of the *New Testament*) one *body* and one *Cup* is propounded to *all*, both Priest and People.

And *Alexander de Hales* reporteth that, when this *lame* and *maimed halfe Communion* was *first* obtruded to the Monasteries, certaine *Monks* took it in high *indignation*, to be depriued

priued of the vse of the *Chalice* or **Cup** of the **Lord**; the rather, becaufe *there is such a comfortable and gracious promise* annexed vnto it; as that, it is the Cup of the New Teftament in Chrifts blood, which is fhed for the *remission of our sinnes.* And verily if it bee the Cup of a *Testament*, giuen vs by *will* in a *Legacie*, they are *false* and perfidious *executors* of Chrifts *laft will* and *Testament*, who fo *facrilegioufly* doe detaine it from the people. *Adulterinum eft, Impium eft, Sacrilegum eft, quodcunque humano furore inftituitur, vt difpofitio diuina violetur. Procul ab huius modi, &c.* It is *adulterous*, it is impious, it is *sacrilegious*, whatfoeuer is eftablifhed by the *fury & madneffe of Man*, to violate and *breake* the Inftitution and *ordinance*

A Preparation

dinance of God. *Fly* ye from the *contagion* of such kinde of men, and by flying away labour to auoid their *communications*, as ye would shun the *Plague* or *infection*; saith Saint *Cyprian*. *Indignus est Domino, qui aliter celebrat hoc Mysterium, quàm ab eo traditum est. Non enim potest Deuotus esse, qui aliter præsumit, quàm datum est ab Authore.* Hee is *vnworthy* of the Lord, which doth *celebrate this Mysterie* otherwise *then it was deliuered by him.* For *he cannot be deuout or religious, who dath presume to giue it otherwise, then it was giuen by the Author.*

But I leaue *them* to the *Lord*, whose *Testament* they doe *violate* in bereauing his *redeemed* of the *Legacy* of his *blood*: and so I proceed to another Name of this Sacrament, which wee may

Cyprian ad Felicem Epist. 8.

Ambros. in 1.Cor.11.

3

may gather out of Scripture: that is, a Commemoration of Christ. Doe *this* in *remembrance of me.* Tis true that this Sacrament is the *Commemoration of Christs* death and Passion *principally*: but it is *not only* of his Death, but *of other actions* and mysteries of Christ also. For as *one* said very wittily, that *Passio Christi est Epitome totius Legis.* The *Passion* of Christ is the *Epitome* or *compendious Abridgement* of the *whole Law of Moses;* so we may *truely say,* that *this Sacrament* of Christ his body & blood is the *short Compendium* or Abridgement of the *whole Gospell* of Christ.

1. Cor. 11.24.

1 For if we begin with the *Conception* and *Incarnation* of Christ, wee shall finde a great *affinitie* and *correspondency* betwixt

twixt *that*, and *this*. For as the *internall* and *eternall Word* of God comming to the *Humane Nature* of Christ, *Verbum caro factum est*, the *Word was made flesh*. So the *externall* and *Temporall* Word of God comming to the *elements* of Bread and Wine, of *them twaine*, vnited together, is made this *diuine Sacrament*, according to the *assertion* of Saint *Augustin*, *Accedat verbum ad Elementum, & fit Sacramentum*. Let the *word of God come* (or, bee added) *to the earthly element*, and *then it is made a Sacrament*. For the element of *Water* in Baptisme, or of *Bread and Wine* in the Lords Supper, are *not Sacraments* (not *Organs* and *instruments* to conuey the *grace of* Christ vnto *vs*) except the *Word of God* be first ioyned vnto

Ioh.1.14.

to them: That is, vnlesse *they bee hallowed* with the *Word of Gods promise*, and *with Prayer*. In which regard the *Church of England* doth straightly enioyne; that *no bread or Wine newly brought* (to the Church, or Communion Table) *shall be vsed*; but, first *the words of Institution shall be rehearsed, when the said Bread and Wine be present vpon the Communion Table*. Which *Ordinance* I could *wish* were *more duely* obserued by *some* Ministers, then in *many places* it is. For *they*, in diuers places, as soone as *new bread* or *new wine* is brought into the *Church* out of the Tauerne, doe make no bones to *administer* it to the *communicants* there present; albeit they doe *neuer* rehearse the words of *institution* ouer the said new Wine or new

Constitut. & can. Eccles Can. 21.

A Preparation

new Bread. Wherein first they transgresse against the *law* established: secondly, they *mocke* the people, making them to *beleeue* that they administer a *Sacrament* to them, when in *truth* they administer *none*, but *common bread* and *common wine*; such as haue *no more power* to conuey the *body and blood of Christ* to mens *soules*, then the *bread* and *wine* at an *ordinarie Table*: and the *reason* is, because *Gods name* is not *inuocated* vpon them, nor the *promise of Christ* in his institution annexed vnto them. For not the *word alone*, nor the *elements alone*, but the *word* ioyned to the *elements*, do make a *Sacrament*: as not the *Godhead alone*, or the *Manhood alone* do make *Christ*, but the *Godhead* and *Manhood* ioyned and vnited both together. More-

Moreouer, as by the *personall* and *hypostaticall vnion* of the Godhead with the flesh, & *humanity* of Christ, it comes to passe that God is Man, and Man God: so by the *sacramentall vnion* of the *body* and *blood* of Christ with the *consecrated Elements* of *bread* and *wine*, it commeth to passe, that the *sacramentall bread* is Christ his *body*, and the *sacramentall wine* his *blood*, (as I touched before.)

Besides, howsoeuer that the *personall vnion* of the Sonne of God to our *Nature* in his *Incarnation*, was very *neere*, and is the *first great mystery of godlinesse, God manifested in the flesh.* 1 *Tim.* 3.16. Yet notwithstanding, wee may bee bold to say, that the *vnion* which passeth betwixt *Christ and vs* in this *sacra-*

Sacrament doth surpasse *that* in two respects.

First, that *personall and hypostaticall vnion*, it was the *coniunction* of *God* and *mans nature* in *generall*: but *this* comes *neerer*, and doth incorporate *our particular persons* into one body with Christ. Howsoeuer the *other* in his *owne nature*, be great, betweene the *things* themselues vnited; yet neuertheleffe this is *vnto vs* more comfortable; becaufe it brings with it a *particular application* to euery one. So that *wee* may pray and say with *Dauid, Psal.* 35.3. *Say vnto* my soule, *I am* thy *saluation*: Not onely saluation to *all* in generall, but to *thy soule* and *my soule* in particular; which is much *more comfortable*.

Therefore God hath for this pur-

purpose not onely ordained the *preaching* of the Gospell in *publique*, to declare the loue of God in Christ Iesus to *mankind* in generall: but hee hath also instituted Sacraments, which are ministred to *euerie* ones person in *particular*. That as Gods loue is vnto all, so hee might seale and confirme the same to euery particular person that is capable of it. *Roffen. in Cant.* 8.6.

Hence it is that Saint *Chrysostome* calleth the Eucharist, *Incarnationis extensionem*, the extension or stretching out of Christ *his Incarnation*. For the *mystery* of the Incarnation was limited & confined to *the person* of our Sauiour *Christ*, (for the Diuinity was not vnited personally to any but to him) but *in this Sacrament* it doth

doth dilate and *extend it selfe* so farre, that it seemeth to be willing (after a sort) to bee incarnate, and to be *whole* in *all*, and to become *one* and the *selfesame thing* with them.

Secondly, this *mysticall* coniunction doth excell *that hypostaticall* vnion in *this*: That though Christ did take our *nature* vpon *him*, and our *Nature* with all *humane infirmities*; yet hee did take *it* cleane *from all sinne*. But in *this mystical vnion* betwixt Christ and his members (though *we* be full of *sinne* and infirmities, as well in soule, as body) yet he vouchsafeth to *knit vs to himselfe*, as being *one bodie*. Which *vnion* is most comfortably set downe in Scripture by *two Metaphors*. It is expressed by the *head* & the *members*; and by the *Husband* and

and *Wife*. But *Nero*, or some other *Tyrant* may chop the *head* from the *members*; and *death* may make a *separation* betwixt *man* and *wife*: But of *this union*, saith S. *Paul*, *I am perswaded that neither death, nor life, nor powers*, nor *principalities shal be able to separate vs from Christ*. [Rom 8.28. Ro.Fen.ibid.]

Secondly, *this Sacrament* hath a *correspondency* with the *Natiuity* of Christ. The circumstance of *time* agrees. For Christ was *borne* in the *night time*, Luke 2.8. and he instituted this Sacrament in the *night season* too. *In the same night that he was betrayed he tooke bread*. [1 Cor. 11.23.] And as *then* Christ hauing taken flesh of the substance of the *blessed Virgin*, was borne of her wombe: So in a *sacramentall manner* he is born of the *substance of bread and wine*;

wine; when as by a *mysticall & inutterable conuersion*, his body is *sacramentally* made of the substance of bread, & his blood of the wine. *There* he was born in *Bethlem*, the *house of bread*, and *here* he is borne in the *house of bread* too.

To this I adde; that Christ hath a *threefold Natiuity*. The first, is *eternall*; the second, *temporall*; the third, *spirituall*. As hee is *God*, hee is borne of his *Father* without a *Mother*, eternally: as he is *Man*, he is borne of his *Mother*, without a *Father*, temporally: In the soule of a *iust man*, as his *particular Sauiour*, he is borne *spiritually*. In the *soule* he is conceiued *per affectum*, by affection; he is born *per effectum*, by effecting and working: he groweth *per profectum*, by profiting and going for-

forward in the wayes of godlinesse.

Of his *Father* he is born *God the Creator*: of his *Mother*, he is borne God-~~Man~~, the man *Redeemer*: of the godly *soule*, he is borne *God*, the *iustifier*. Of his *Father*, he is borne *sublimitie and Maiestie*: of his *mother* he is borne *lowlinesse* and *humilitie*: of the pious *soule* he is borne *mercy and verity*. For hee confirmeth his *mercy* and *truth* by the Sacrament to *euery soule* that *receiues* him *truely*. Wherefore, then the Church doth sing; vnto *vs a Child is Borne, and vnto vs a Sonne is giuen*. How *rich* therefore are *we made* in Him. *Qui possessorem Omniũ habet, in illo cuncta possidet*: who so hath the owner and *possessor of all things*, *doth* in him *possesse all things*.

Esay 9.

3 Let vs proceed forward to his *preſentation* in the *Temple* at the feaſt of the *Purification*, and we ſhall plainely confeſſe; that as, at that time, hee was preſented to bee *offered* to the Eternall Father, as an *Innocent Lambe:* ſo *here* is repreſented the fleſh and blood of the *Lambe of God*, which offered himſelfe to God, *to take away the ſinnes of the world.*

Luke 2.22.

4 Then if wee caſt our eyes vpon *that* which dazeled the *eyes* of his bleſſed Apoſtles, *Peter, Iames,* and *Iohn*; that is, vpon his *transfiguration* vpon Mount *Tabor*: Euen as Chriſt being *then transfigured,* did not loſe his *former nature,* or *naturall figure*: ſo *here*, albeit the *bread* and *wine* (after the words of *conſecration,* and ſolemn *Benediction*) are *changed* & altered from

Luke 9.

from what *they were* before: (for whereas *before* they were *common bread* and *common wine*, and were *naturall* instruments and *meanes* to preserue *naturall life*; *now* (being hallowed and sanctified, by the speciall *promise of God* and *prayer*) they become the *sacramentall body and blood of Christ*, and are made *morall instruments*, to conuey vnto vs the *fruits* of Christ his *body* and *blood*, and to feed vs to *eternall life*.) Yet are they not *so changed* and *altered* (*in regard of vse,*) but that they doe *still* retaine the *nature* and *naturall qualities*, which they had before. Wherfore, euen *after consecration*, Saint *Paul* is not afraid *three seuerall times to call it bread*.

And, as when Christ was *transfigured*, there was a commemoration

1.Cor.11.26, 17,18.

memoration of his *death*, For *Loquebantur de excessu*, they *talked of his departure* and *suffering*, which hee should *accomplish at Hierusalem*. So at the *Institution* of this Sacrament, *Christ* made mention of his *suffering* too: (This is *my bodie* which is *broken for you*: This *Cup* is the *New Testament in my blood*, which *is shed for you* and for many for the remission of sins) and as *then* hee did make mention of his owne death; so hath hee left a *charge* vpon the *Church* to do the like alwaies *at the celebration of this Supper*. *Hoc facite in Commemorationem mei*: Do this in *remembrance* of me.

5 But if wee goe on to his *Death & Passion*, we shall see it *most liuely* described *euen before our eyes*. For the *breaking of the bread* & the *powring* out of the *wine*

Luke 9.31.

wine doth signifie & represent the *breaking* of his *body* and the shedding of his *blood*; the *separatiō* of his *soule* frō his *flesh*, which was at his death. *For so often as we eate this bread and drinke this Cup, we doe declare the Lords death til he come.* And therupon *Austin* saith, that the Supper of the Lord is a *Sermon*, and the Priest *therein preacheth* and vttereth *the death of the Lord.*

As Christ at his Passion did *patiently subiect* himselfe to the seuerity and cruelty of his persecutors and *executioners*, insomuch that *by them* he suffered himselfe to bee nayled to the *Crosse*: so in this *diuine Sacrament* he hath *subiected* himselfe to many *impious disgraces, scornes,* and *iniuries* which are done to him by *sacrilegious, wicked, vnsanctified,* and *vnworthy*

1. Cor. 11. 26.

Aug. de Trinit. lib. 3. cap. 4.

thy Communicants. *Men* comming to eate his body and drinke his blood, with *hearts full of treacherie, hatred, rancour, vncleannesse*; with *eyes full of Adultery* and *Envy, pride* and *haughtinesse*; with *heads full of wicked* and *vngodly imaginations*; with *hands full of Rapine, Extortion, Oppression, iniustice*: *with feet swift to shed blood, destruction and vnhappinesse being in their wayes*, nor they being acquainted with the way of Peace. So that, they *doe crucifie againe the Sonne of God.* Hence it is, that Saint *Augustine,* in *one* of his Sermons, doth *bring in Christ* complaining of the grieuous wrongs, wherewith *he is burdened* euery day by *vnworthy Receiuers* (in this manner.) *Cur me grauiori criminum tuorum* Cruci, quàm

Heb. 6.

Aug. Serm. 181.

quàm illa, in quâ olim pependeram affixisti? Grauior enim apud me peccatorum crux est, in quâ inuitus pendeo, quàm illa in quam tui misertus ascendi. Why dost thou *nayle* me to thy *sins Crosse*, which is *more grieuous* to me then that *wooden Crosse* whereon I hanged in *times past?* For the Gibbet or Crosse of thy *sinnes* or *offences*, on which I hang *sore against my will*, is much *more grieuous* and vnsufferable to *mee*, then was that *Crosse*, which I, *taking pitty on thee, did ascend vpon* of mine owne accord.

6 And for his Resurrection. Who knoweth not that by it, he that *humbled* himselfe to the *lowest*, euen to the *death* of the *Crosse*, was *super exaltatus*, most *highly exalted* aboue all: so in this Sacrament, the *poore elements*

A Preparation

ments of bread and wine which in *themselues* doe appeare but poore contemptible things, after *consecration*, are exalted to such an *high honour*, that they represent the highest mysteries of our Religion.

7 And it hath some resemblance to his *ascension*. For as Christ by his ascension, did *ouer-mount* all *created natures*, and put them vnder his feet; so our soule being sustained and supported by this diuine food, doth not *onely surmount all things created*, by an holy contempt and scorne; but *Elias-like*, by this heauenly refection, doth put on a *fresh strength* and *alacrity*, to cary vs to the top of the Mount *Horeb*; that is, to *eternall beatitude*.

And as Christ at his ascension, *appeared before God for vs,* Heb.

Heb. 9. to become our *Intercessor* and *Aduocate*, (*For we haue an Aduocate with the Father, Iesus* Christ *the righteous, &c.* 1 *Iohn* 2.) So at the *participation of this Sacrament*, we may be *sure* that Christ, *seeing the commemoration of his death and passion* duly performed, *doth plead for our pardon* and remission, by vertue of his *precious blood-shedding.*

8 In this Sacrament wee haue Christ his *comming to iudgement* presented vnto *vs.* And therefore in *ancient times* it was called *Hally-doome.* That is, *holy doome* or *holy iudgment:* because a man was to *iudge himselfe* guilty, or guiltlesse, *condemned* or *acquitted*, according to his *worthy* or *vnworthy receiuing* of the same. Hee that eateth or drinketh *vnworthily, eateth*

1 Cor. 11 23.

eateth and drinketh his owne damnation. Or, as others will haue it, *He eateth and drinketh Iudgement to himselfe.* And, if we would *iudge our selues,* we should *not be iudged. Verſ.* 31.

9 It is also a *kind of resemblance* of the *descension of the Holy-Ghost.* For as the Holy-Ghost at *Pentecost* did both sanctifie and strengthen the minds of the Apostles: so this *Sacrament,* being duly receiued; doth make the *communicants* more *carefull* for the *correction of their liues,* and doth more *plentifully enrich* them with *cœlestiall gifts and endowments.*

10 In it is a representation of the *holy Catholique Church,* and of the *communion of Saints.* For so the Apostle teacheth vs in 1 Cor. 10. 16. 17. *The cup of blessing which we blesse, it is not the*

Cum ſaturati fuerint, vide quid agant; intellige quid loquantur; quàm ſancti odoris ſit, quicquid illa eructat plenitudo, verbum bonum mores cōpoſitos, affectus pudicos, ſenſus pacificos. Cyprian Serm. de Cœnâ Dom.

to the Sacrament.

the *Communion of the blood of Christ?* The *bread* which wee break, is it *not the Comunion of the body of* Christ? For we, *that are many*, are *one Bread*, and *one body*; because we al are *partakers of one bread*. So it is said in the *Thanksgiuing*, at the *end* of the Psalme Booke.

———As the *cornes*, by vnity into *one loafe* is knit,
So is the *Lord* and his *whole Church*, though *he* in heauē sit.
As *many* Grapes make but *one* wine, so should *we* bee but *One*:
In faith and loue, in Christ aboue, and vnto Christ alone.

11 The next Article, that followes, is the *remißion of sins*: And doth not *euery child* know that this Sacrament was instituted

tuted to *assure our soules* of the free *remission* of our sinnes thorow the *blood of Christ?* *This Cup is the new Testament in my blood, which was shed for the remission of sins. Mat. 26. 28.*

12 And concerning the *resurrection of the body*, and *life euerlasting*; our Sauiour hath told vs plainly enough, *Iohn 6. 54. Whosoeuer eateth my flesh & drinketh my blood, hath eternall life, and I will raise him vp at the last day.*

Wherefore, let vs *thus come* to the table of the Lord, *thus* let vs eat of that bread, & drink of that cup, holding an immouable confession of our hope. That is, a stedfast and *vnwauering expectation* to obtaine eternall blessednesse by the benefit of so *great a gift*. For assuredly, he that hath *giuen vs his owne*

owne flesh and blood, will neuer deny vs the *inheritance which he hath promised*. Hee hath left vs a most *vndoubted pledge and pawne* to assure vs ; besides, hee which hath *promised vs, is faithfull*, so that we haue no reason to stagger or wauer ; hauing so *sure a pledge*, so *faithfull a promiser*. What saith his promise; *He that eateth my flesh, &c. hath eternall life ; and I will raise him vp at the last day*. Now, *at this instant*, hee hath eternall life *in his soule* ; and *hereafter*, at the last day, that he may haue his *perfect consummation* and *blessednesse both in body and soule*, I, to *whom* hee hath adhered ; I, who haue *incorporated him* into my selfe, by my *holy Sacraments*, because *I am Life*, I will enlifen and raise vp him (that is, *his body*) at the last day ; that
being

being wholly blessed both in *soule* and *body*, he with the *glorious Angels* may enioy the *gracious* and euer comfortable aspect of my *countenance*, for euerlasting, in my *court of heauen*.

So much shall suffice for the *names* that it hath in Scripture. In the Fathers also it hath diuers appellations. But I touch but vpon three: viz. that it is called a *Sacrifice*, the *Eucharist*, and the *Sacrament*; as it were, κατ' ἐξοχὴν by a kind of *excellence*:

1 The Fathers most ordinarily, when they make mention of the Supper of the Lord, doe terme it a *sacrifice*, an *Host*, an *Oblation*, &c. Whereupon (by *wrested* and wrong *interpretations*) the Papists do build their Sacrifice of the *Masse*: wherein the

the *Priest* doth, as they say, offer to God the Sacrifice of Christs *body* and *blood, pro vivis & defunctis*, for the quicke and the dead; and as a *propitiation for sinnes, &c*. They say that they doe really and corporally sacrifice the Son of God vnder the *formes of bread and wine*; and that the Priests Act (though the *people* neither *vnderstand* what he *saith*, nor *know* what he *doth*, but *gaze* on him, whilest hee alone murmureth to himselfe in a *Tongue vnknown*, and maketh that *private to one*, that should be *common to all* by Christs institution) is notwithstanding *very profitable* before God, for such as doe hire his *paines*, or please his *humour*, to be had in mind, when he rubbeth his memory. *Bils. ad Apolog.Ies.part.4.pag.701.*

But

But in the writings of the *ancient Fathers* it is called a *sacrifice* in other regards, and not in that which the Papists doe *feigne.* First, because it is a *commemoration* of the *sacrifice* of Christ offered vpon the Crosse; and a *thanksgiuing* for that Sacrifice. Which *thanksgiuing* is a *sacrifice*, as S. *Paul* teacheth vs, *Heb.* 13.15. *Let vs therefore by him offer the sacrifice of praise* alwayes to God.

And for this cause it is called *Euchariſtia*, the *Eucharist*, which signifieth *giuing of thankes.* Therefore immediately after the *Lords Prayer* recited (when wee are to conclude the *Communion*) the Booke of *Common Prayer* teacheth vs to say thus, *Wee thine humble seruants* entirely desire thy fatherly goodnesse mercifully to accept

cept this *our sacrifice of praise and thanksgiving.*

Secondly, it is called a *sacrifice*, because euery faithful *Communicant* doth present *his body and soule* to be a holy liuing and *acceptable sacrifice* vnto God. For as *in this Sacrament* God doth *offer* Christ, with all his merits and benefits *vnto vs*: so wee, on the other side, doe *offer* vp *our selues*, our soules and bodies, *wholly to God*, promising him that wee will *walke henceforward in his holy wayes*.

Thirdly, it is *so called*: because at *the celebration* of the Lords Supper, there was *a certaine collection made of the Almes of the people*, for the vse of the poore. For *Almes-deeds*, done to the *poore* members of Christ for the *loue* that wee owe to Christ, are *sacrifices* very pleasing

Communion Booke, ibid.

sing and acceptable to God.

Fourthly, becauſe the *body* of Chriſt is offered in the *holy Supper*, after *a ſort*. Firſt, as the *bread* is the *body* of Chriſt *ſacramentally*: ſo the *breaking* of the bread is the *immolation* or *ſacrificing* of Chriſt vpon the Croſſe *ſacramentally*. Secondly, *Chriſt* in the Sacrament of the Supper is *offered vp* in *reſpect* of the *faith* of ſuch as doe *communicate*; who, by *their faith*, doe preſent and *ſet before their eyes* things *done and paſt*, as if they were *now* preſent and *in doing*.

Concerning the *former*, S. *Auguſtine* ſaith, *Nonne ſemel immolatus eſt Chriſtus? & tamen in Sacramento, &c.* was not Chriſt offered vp in ſacrifice once onely? and yet in the Sacrament, not onely at *all Eaſter*

ster-*solemnities*, but *every day* hee is *offered* for the people. *Neither doth hee speake any vntruth*; who, being asked, *shall answer* that *Christ is slaine* and *offered in sacrifice*. For if the *Sacraments* should not haue a *certaine similitude* of those *things* whereof they be *Sacraments*, they should *then* bee *no Sacraments at all*. For *by reason* of *this similitude* and correspondence, *they doe*, for the most part, *receiue the names* of the *very things* themselues.

Concerning the *second*. The same Saint *Augustine* saith, *Tum immolatum fuisse Christū pro nobis, cum in eum Credimus.* Christ was *then* offered vp in sacrifice for *vs*, when *wee doe* beleeue in him. And, againe: *Tum pro vnoquoq; mortuus est Christus, quando pro se mortuum*

August. ad Bonif. Epist. 23.

esse illum certò persuasus est. Then *is Christ dead* for euery man; *when a man is certainly perswaded that he died for him.*

So that, to speake as it is in *deed* and in *truth*, the Lords Supper is not *Sacrificium ἱλαστικὸν, sed εὐχαριστικὸν*; not properly a *Sacrifice* of *propitiation* for sinnes: but a *sacrifice* of *praise & thanksgiuing*, a thankfull *recordation* and commemoration of the *sacrifice*, which Christ *offered for vs vpon the* Crosse. Whence it is that Saint *Augustine* said. *Sacrificium panis et vini Ecclesia offerre non cessat. In isto autem sacrificio, Gratiarum actio atque commemoratio est Carnis Christi quam pro nobis obtulit, &c.*

The *Church* doth not *leaue off* to offer the *sacrifice of bread and wine.* And in *that sacrifice* there

August. lib 2. quæst. vet. & Nou. Testamen. ad Roman.

Aug. de fide ad Petrum Diaconum cap. 19.

there is a *rendring of thankes*, and a *commemoration* of the *flesh* of Christ, which hee offered for *vs*; and of the *blood*, which he *shed for vs*. And *Peter Lumbard* also treadeth in the same steps. For the *Lords Table* in respect of *his graces* and mercies *there* proposed, is an *heauenly banquet*, which *we* must *eate*, and not *sacrifice*. But the *duties* which *hee* requireth at *our* hands when *wee* approach to *his Table* are *sacrifices*, not *Sacraments*: as namely, to offer him *thanks* and *praise*, *faith*, *obedience*, yea, our *soules* and *bodies* to be a liuing and acceptable sacrifice to him.

<small>Lumbard. lib. 4. Distinct. 12.</small>

<small>B. Bilson ibid. pag. 699.</small>

It is called the *Eucharist*, as it hath beene touched *before*. And it is therefore so called, as *Chrysostom* (in his 16 Homilie in *Matthæum*) explaines it: be-

P 3   cause

A Preparation

cause in the celebration of this Sacrament, there is to euery Communicant, propounded a consideration of the manifold and various benefits of Almighty God bestowed vpon vs: and *principally*, of the *prime worke of the loue of God towards vs*, in that he *sent* his onely *Sonne*, who by *yeelding* vp his *body* to bee *sacrificed* vpon the Crosse, and by *effusion* of his *blood*, redeemed *vs*, when we perished & were *lost* : That *so* we might be inuited and incited to render our *heartiest thankes* to God for the same. Now this *sacrifice* of *praise* and thanksgiuing is often comended in Scripture: *who so offereth me thankes and praise, he honoreth me.*

Psal. 50.26.
Heb. 13.

And whereas, at the *end of* the *Communion*, wee sing and say

say that *Hymne* of glory, (*Glory be to God on High, & on earth peace, and good will towards men; we praise thee, wee blesse thee, we glorifie thee,&c.*) the *Fathers* doe call such *solemne songs* of *praise* and *thanks, sacrifices*; As *Aug:* saith. And the *Greeke Cannon* makes expresse mention of the *Hymne of glory*.

Aug. Epist. 120.

But the *Papists* (many times) doe *expressely* distinguish *their sacrifice of the Masse*, from the *Sacrament* of the *Eucharist*. The *Masse* is *offred* by the *Priest alone*: and *he* doth participate vnder *both kinds*: but the Sacrament of the *Eucharist* is distributed to the *people*; and *that* but vnder *one* onely *kinde*; vnder the *forme* of *Bread*; the *Cup* being restrained from *them*. Because, as they say, the *blood* of Christ is *in* his *body*; and

P 4   who

who so receiueth the *body*, receiueth the *blood, per cōcomitantiam*: because the blood doth euer *concomitate* the body. But I see no reason why it should not *concomitate* in the *sacrifice* of the *Masse*, as well as in the *Sacrament* of the *Eucharist*. For *Duæ species requiruntur ad sacrificium: sed ad essentiam Sacramenti, quælibet, ex duabus, sufficit.* Both the *kinds* of bread and wine are required to the *sacrifice* of the *Masse*: but either of *both* is sufficient for the *Sacrament*. And *Gropperus* was somewhat ill *handled* at the *Councell of Trent*, because *hee* said that the *Sacrament of the Eucharist* or the *Cōmunion* was *de substantiâ sacrificij Missæ*; of the very *substance* of the *sacrifice* of the *Masse*. *Quasi maneat præ foribus concomitantia, sacrificante*

Bellar. in Apol. contra. præf. moniter. pag. 802.

Chemn. exam. Conc. Trid. Sess. 5. cap. 4.

crificante, *&c.* As if *concomitance*, all the while the Priest were in *sacrificing* the Masse, did stand *without doores*: but as soone as that was *ended*, and he going to the *sacrament*, then it were called *in*. As that *liuing Library* and *Non sicut* of inuention and iudgement, the *now Lord Bishop of Winchester* saith; in *Respons. ad Apol. Cardin. Bellar. pag.* 186.

For the *Sacrament*, being nothing but a *participation* of the *Sacrifice* (for in the *Lords supper* there is a *pacificall* and *Euchuaristicall* Sacrifice) Consider Israel which is after the flesh; are not those which eate of the *sacrifice* pertakers of the Altar? *1 Cor.* 10. 18.

As the Sacrifice is not *whole* (but *maimed*) vnlesse the *body* be *broken*, and except the *blood* be be powred out: so there cannot be an entire and full *participation* of the *sacrifice*, vnlesse a man doe partake of *both*; not *onely* of the *body broken*, but also of the *blood* powred out. The Apostle there noteth the *Symbole* of the *body*, by the *bread* which we *breake*; and, of the *blood*, by the *cup* which we *blesse*. 1 *Cor*.10.16. The *bread* is the *participation* of the bodie; the *cup* is the *communion* of the *blood*: as the same *right Reuerend Father* hath most learnedly obserued.

But (not to dwell longer vpon those *sacrilegious absurdities* of the Papists) if this Sacrament be an *Eucharist*, that is, a *rendring* of *thankes* and *praise* to God for his infinit mercies, in sauing our bodies and soules from hell-fire, and for many other

to the Sacrament.

ther *vnualuable* benefits, which our *Saviour* did purchase *for vs* by his death and blood-shedding: then certainly it cannot *more decently* be receiued then vpon our knees. If we could bow our knees *so low* as *hell*, we could not bow them *low enough* to testifie the infinit thankes and praise which wee owe to God for his innumerable and inestimable benefits *conferred* vpon vs, and sealed vnto vs *in* and *by* this Sacrament. If wee were to receiue a *great fauour* from our Soueraigne, wee could not *receiue* it nor render *thankes* for it, *more fitly and beseemingly* then on our *knees*. Alas! then why should *any* of the *Children* of our *Church* jangle and brangle with *vs* about *kneeling* at this Sacrament? Can wee giue

thankes

thankes to God for the *redemption* of our soules from eternall death, by the *precious death* of his deare Sonne, in any *lesse humble* manner then by *kneeling* on our knees? is it *so seemly* or *lesse vnmannerly* to receiue it *sitting*, as if wee were *hayle fellow well met*, with the God of incomprehensible Maiesty and Glory? But, *Dum vitant stulti, &c.* Weake brain'd men, whilest they seek to auoyd *one error*, doe often fall into *another*, which is as *bad*, if not *worse*. Because the *Papists* by some are taxed for *Idolatry*, in giuing vndue *Adoration* to the *consecrated Host*, the sacramentall Bread: therefore *some others*, because they would shunne all *shew* of idolatry, are so farre from *adoring* the *bread*, that they will not *kneele* downe to God,

God, and *adore him* for his incomprehensible fauours and benefits, and blessings exhibited and conferred vpon *them.* But I will take my finger from off *that Byle,* and proceed vnto the *last name,* which I propounded to be giuen by the *Fathers,* to this Sacrament.

It is called by them *the Sacrament,* by a kind of ἐξοχὴν, or *excellence*: in *comparison* of the Sacraments of the *Old Testament.*

Whereupon *Dionysius (in Cælesti Hierarchiâ)* calleth it *Cæterorum consummationem;* the perfection and *consummation of the rest*: All the Sacraments of the Old Testament, (their *Manna,* their *Paschall Lambe,* yea, *the Tree of life* in Paradise) are recapitulate in *this.*

But

A Preparation

But I pitch onely vpon the very word (*Sacramentum*) which in one of its most natiue and original significations doth signifie an *oath*. For here is a *solemne bond* of an oath passed betwixt Gods and vs. Wherein God doth graciously *bind him* by his *word of promise*, and ☙ the *seale* of his Sonnes most precious Body & Blood, to giue vnto vs *free pardon* and remission of all our sinnes, and *all other benefits* of his death & passion, vpon our worthy receiuing of it: And *we* on the other side, doe *bind* our selues by *oath and vow* to God, that (as we hope for pardon and remission of our sinnes, or to haue *any share* in the Body & Blood of Christ) we will *turne ouer a new leafe*, become *new men*, and from *thence forward* walke in obe-

obedience to his *holy lawes* and *Commandements* all the dayes of our life: that is, Seeing God hath beene so gracious vnto vs, as to deliuer vs from that κατάκριμα, the *penalty* or *curse* of euerlasting condemnation due vnto vs, (which is the *correctiue* part of the Law) we therfore doe *bind our selues* to fulfill δικαίωμα τȣ Νόμȣ, the righteousnesse of the Law, by ordering and squaring our liues according to the *directiue* part of the Law.

We are not by *the sacrament* to bind our selues to commit horrible and grieuous sins (in *blowing vp Parliaments, poysoning & stabbing of Kings, murthering of Innocents*, and such like) but to bind our selues from working or committing any wickednesse. For so did the

true

true *Christians* in the *Primitive* Church; as it is left vpon record by one of their *persecutors*, euen by *Plinius Secundus* in an Epistle to *Trajanus* the Emperour: where he giueth this testimony of them: viz. This was the *maine*, whether of their offence or error, namely, that *they* were wont vpon a *set day*, (that *set day* was *Sunday*) to *meet together* before the Sunne was vp, and to sing amongst themselues an *Hymne* or *Psalm* to Christ, as to God; and to *bind* themselues by an *oath* or *sacrament*, Not to commit any wickednesse: but, *Ne furta, ne latrocinia, &c.* to tye themselues from committing *thefts*, or *robberies*, or *adulteries*, from *breach of promise*, from *betraying of trust, &c.* That is, they bound themselues from breaking

Affirmabant autem hanc fuisse summam vel culpæ suæ, vel erroris; quòd essent soliti stato die ante lucem conuenire: Carmeńq; Christo, quasi Deo, dicere secum inuicem: seq; Sacramento, non in scelus aliquod obstringere, sed, Ne furta, Ne latrocinia, Ne adulteria committerent, Ne fidem fallerent, &c. C. Plin. Cæc. Secund lib. 10. Epist. 97.

to the Sacrament.

ing of *Gods Law*, and obliged themselues to *fulfill* the *righteousnesse thereof*; by *leading a new life, & walking from thenceforth in his holy wayes.*

The second *thing* to be considered in *Faith*, is *Application.* Therefore euery Communicant must not onely *know*, but *apply* that in *particular* to himselfe, which he *beleeueth* in *generall*: as that Christs *body* was crucified *for him*, and his *blood* shed *for him.* S. Paul teacheth it by his *owne example, I liue,* saith he, *by the faith of the Sonne of God, who hath loued mee, and hath giuen himselfe for me.* And this *Application* cannot be better performed, then in *eating this bread*, and *drinking this Cup:* for so often as we eat this Bread, and drinke this Cup we doe Commemorate the Lords

Gal.2.20.

1.Cor.11.26.

Q   Death

Death. Every Communion is as it were, a *new Crucifixion* of Chrift. Chrift was crucified *at Hierufalem*: but Saint *Paul* tels the *Galatians*, that hee was crucified *among them*. Not that hee fuffered death *in Galatia*; but becaufe *of the Communion*: which is a Commemoration and *Reprefentation of the Death and Paſſion of Chrift*.

Gal.3.1.

Therefore when I kneele at the Lords Table (to the end that I more effectually apply Chrift to mine owne Soule) I *am to fet my felfe* as it were at the very *foot of Chrift his croſſe*, and to confider *Him* hanging there, enduring the vnknowne wrath and curfe of God, and fhedding his moft precious blood *for me* and *for my finnes*. That I *was* the caufe why *Hee* was *wounded*, rent, torne, and moft most shamefully vsed; That *my sinnes murthered* the glorious and innocent *Sonne of God*; that he suffered *nothing for his owne sake*, but all for *mine*: that he sustained his *Fathers wrath* to turne that wrath *away* from me; and to make *God and mee friends*: that hee was content to be made a *Curse* to *saue* mee from the curse, and make mee *blessed*: that he suffered *shame*, to *saue mee* from shame, and *crowne* me with *glory*, &c.

And *there* (at the Communion Table) am I *so* to collect and *gather vp my* stragling thoughts, that (*shutting out* of my mind al other cogitations) I am so to settle my selfe, as if *none* were there present, but the blessed Trinity and I my selfe. *God* the Father, who is the *person offended*: *I*, who am the offender;

fender; and *Christ*, who hangs on the Crosse, as my *Pawn* and *Surety*, to pay my *Debt*; suffering *all that* which is due *vnto mee*.

And if I aske the reason, why *God* gaue his *Sonne* to doe and suffer *all this* for my sake, or why the *Sonne* of God *would* suffer it? I shall finde *none*, but the great and *infinite loue* to *me*, who deserued no loue at all; but rather *all hatred and vengeance* from them.

It was in God his incomprehensible loue, that caused him to *giue his* Sonne *to me*, and *for me*. *God so loued the world, that he gaue his onely begotten Sonne, &c. This loue* of Gods, is a *Sic* without any *Sicut*; beyond all comparison: nothing that euer was, or shall bee, may stand in comparison with it. God *so* loued

Iohn 3.16.

ued the world, that he gaue his onely begotten Sonne. It is as much (saith S. *Augustine*) as if some *mighty Monarch*, who had but *one* only *Sonne*, should haue in his Kingdom a miserable *poore subiect*, falne into a desperate disease, that were *not curable* by any meanes in the world, but *by washing himselfe in a Bath made of the blood of the yong Prince*: And the *King shuld* so far tender the health of that *poore Snake*, that (hauing but *one Sonne*, and him the *Hope* of his posteritie, and *Heire* of his Kingdome) hee should cause *all* his veynes to bee opened, and all *his blood*, euen to the very *last drop*, to bee emptied out of his *Sons body*, to the losse of his life; and all this, *to saue the life of a mean fellow*, of no parts, or deserts at all. *Such* (saith

Saint

Saint *Auguſtine*) *was the loue of our heauenly Father towards me*, the meaneſt of his ſubiects; he gaue the *life* and *blood* of his onely *deare Sonne*, to cure and heale *mee* a miſerable *wretch*, that otherwiſe had neuer been cured.

A fine and elegant *Compariſon* it is; but yet it commeth ſhort of Gods loue. For the *life* of a *Prince* (though it bee of a very *high price*, in ſo much that the people ſay to *Dauid*, *Thou art worth ten thouſand of vs*) yet the *life of the Sonne of God*, is more worth then the liues of a thouſand millions of Princes. Beſides, the pooreſt *man*, nay the pooreſt *gnat*, in regard of the *greateſt* Prince on the earth, is not ſo meane & *poore*; as the *greateſt* Prince that euer was, is in compariſon of

2 Sam.18.3.

of Gods onely begotten Son. So that *no loue* may be compared to *this loue* of God, in giuing his Sonne *for me*; except it be *the loue of the Sonne* who gaue *himselfe* for me, and *to me*.

God *so* loued *me*, that in respect of *mee*, hee seemed *not to loue* his Sonne: the Sonne *so* loued *me*, that in respect of *me*, he seemed *not to loue himselfe*, but gaue away his *owne life*, to saue *my life*. His death *to me*, is the death of mine *High Priest*; by it I am restored to my *forfeited inheritance in the heauenly Canaan*. His *life and blood* to me, is the life & blood of the *Pelican* in the wildernes; who diggeth her *owne brest*, & sheddeth her blood vpon her yong that are stung with *Serpents*, to restore them to their *health*, though it be with losse

Num.35.28.

Psal.102.

both

both of her *blood* and *life*. His *blood is to me*, not only the *blood of Remission* of sinnes, in *forgiuing*; but *in giuing* vnto me, that which I could neuer haue purchased. It is *Sanguis Testamenti*, the Blood of the Testament; whereby Christ (as in *his Will and Testament*) doth giue and bequeath vnto mee a *Legacie* of Heauen. *His blood* is the blood of *Gods owne* Sonne, the *Heire* of all things in heauen and earth. I doe eate *his flesh*, and *drinke his blood*, and by that am made (hauing the *Blood royall* within me) one of the *blood royall*, and *Sonne* and *Heire* of God, and ioynt-heire with Iesus Christ.

Beneficium postulat officium: Euery benefit doth challenge a dutie at mine hands. And *what* shall I render to the Lord for

for *all these his* benefits? Surely, saith *Dauid*, *I will take the Cup of saluation*, and call vpon the Name of the Lord; that is, giue him thankes and praise, saying, *O my God, thou art good and true!* *O my soule, thou art blessed and happy!* And for this cause, this Sacrament of the Communion is called *Eucharistia*: because it is a *Praise* and *Thanksgiuing* to God, for the vnspeakable benefits which we receiue at his hands, *in* and *by* the Sacrament.

Psal. 116.

But wee must not giue him thanks & praise with *the mouth only*; but to shew that our *hearts* are truely thankefull vnto him, wee must study and endeauor to render *loue for loue*: for *that is all* that hee requires at our hands; *Loue*.

It is recorded by *Xenophon*, that

Lib. 13. Post Cyr.

that that potent and puissant *King* of the *Persians*, *Cyrus* (hauing taken *Tygranes*, *King* of the *Armenians* captiue in war, and led him and his *Queen* prisoners to his owne Court) did vpon a day bid them to his *own Table*; and in a *sport* and merriment, asked of *Tygranes*, *How much he would bestow to ransome his Queene?* He presently made answer; *If I had that kingdome which thou hast wonne from me by the sword, I would willingly part with that to redeeme her; and, if that were not enough, I would spend my life, and powre out my blood for her.* *Cyrus* being strangely taken with the consideration of such excessiue measure of coniugal loue, yearned in compassion towards them, and restored them not onely to their *liberty*, but also to to their *kingdome.* When *Tygranes* was at home in his own *Court*, hee thus bespake his wife the Queene ; *Lady, what doe you thinke of King* Cyrus? *Is not he a most vnmatchable & heroicall King? Is not hee onely worthy to weare the stile and title of a King?* The wise Lady presently made answer : *Sir, I wot not what you say; neither can I remember what King* Cyrus *did say or doe, whereby I might take notice of his wisedome and prudence: for all the while that I (with your selfe) remained a captiue in Persia, I neuer cast mine eyes vpon any one, but vpon him that was resolued to set me at liberty, with the losse and expense of his owne blood.*

    Behold here, a *lesson* taught you frõ this vertuous *Queene*: She acknowledged her selfe to be be *indebted* to her husband *Tygranes*, for that he was purposed to *spend his owne blood for her ransome*, that (for the *vehemency* of loue and affection *towards him*) shee could not endure to looke vpon *any other* in all the *Court* of *Persia*, no, nor vpon *King Cyrus himselfe*.

How *much* then (deare Christians) are you indebted to your *King* & *Spouse*, seeing that he hath not only *purposed* to *redeeme and ransome you* with his *own dearest blood*; but *hath* powred it forth *indeed*, euen vnto the last drop, hauing *for your sake*, suffered so much shame, so many sorrowes, so many torments, to free and ransome *you* from a most *cruel thraldom*, not of the *Persian*, but of *Satan*; and restored you to the free possession, and iust right of a

Cele-

Celestiall kingdome? Can you then look vpon any, can you find in your hearts to *bestow one thought* vpon *any* in the whole court of this world, saue onely vpon your *crucified Lord* and Sauiour Iesus Christ? Cast *all* your thoughts, *all* your looks, *all* your loue vpon him; *Videte & palpate, gustate, & videte*: behold him and feele him, taste and consider him: recognize his *loue to you*, and returne *him loue* againe; *for if any man loue not the Lord Iesus*, let him bee *Anathema Maran-atha*. 2.Cor.16.22.

Now *this* our *loue* cannot better be expressed, then by a *ioiful acknowledgement* of those *wonderfull benefits* which wee receiue from Christ, when we do *worthily* communicate: and a *dutifull obedience* to his commandements. The *later hereof*, Iohn 14. ver. 15.21.24.

is

A Preparation

is (in part) touched before: therefore I will in a word or two, touch vpon the *former*, which is the spirituall and corporall ioy wherwith we should be filled at the time of our receiuing. For the time of Receiuing is not a time of *moody* and *melancholy* passion, but a time of *mirth & ioy* in the Lord. It is *sacrum convivium*; At a *banquet* men ought to bee *very merry*. Our duty then it is to *Reioyce*; onely we are to take heed, that we do not reioice *in sin*, which is *against* the Lord: but *reioyce in the Lord. Reioyce in the Lord alwayes, & againe I say Reioyce.* The *Holy-Ghost* by the Apostle doth not only *permit* and giue leaue to vs to make merry and *reioyce*, but doth *also exhort* vs vnto it. And not *only* to *reioyce*, but to *reioyce againe*. He would haue

A holy banket.

Philip.4:4.

haue our hearts *rauished* with a *double* ioy. *One* for the *soule*, and *another* for the *body*; but *both* in the Lord. So that not only *our soules should bee ioyfull in the Lord, and reioyce in his saluation*, but also our *very bones should* say, *Lord who is like vnto thee?* So that the *bones which thou hast broken may reioyce.*

And certainly we haue *great reason* to reioyce *in God* for his goodnesse to vs. For at the Communion (by the *hands of his Minister*) he doth passe vnto you *vnder seale*, his owne *body and blood*, nay, his *Wholeselfe*, and whatsoeuer *benefit* he wrought for mans saluation: as the *remission* and pardon of all your sinnes; the *redemption* and deliuerance of all your soules and bodies *from eternall punishment* in Hell; *Perfect friend-*

Psal. 51.8.

Psal. 35.9.10.

Friendship, and *Reconciliation* with God; and an *undoubted right* and title to the kingdome of Heauen, with all *the ioyes* and blessednesse thereof.

1 You would *reioyce* and be glad at the heart, if (being indebted but a matter of *twenty*, or *an hundred thousand pounds*, (and not knowing which way to pay it, or any *farthing* of it) you could finde *one* so kind, and *bountifull*, as would pay it *all* for you: and not aske one farthing *backe*, but onely your *true loue, and hearty thankefulnesse.* Beloued, *we* are *all* in *debt*. Our sinnes are *debts* to God: and they are of so *high a nature*, that all the *thousands* and millions in the world are not able to satisfie God *for one of them*; and euery one *of vs are in* for *millions* of thousands: Christ comes

Math. 18. 24.

comes, and brings a *Quietus est*, discharging vs freely of *euery one* of those debts, and passeth it vnder *seale* in the Sacrament; and haue wee not *farre greater* cause to reioyce for this, then for *the other?* For his blood, is the blood of Remission of sinnes.

2 If any of you had offended *the Law* in any heinous manner, and for that (being *legally* adiudged to death) had the *Halter* about his *neck*, vpon the *Gallowes*, being ready to be *turned off* the Ladder; would it not glad his heart, to see one come from *the King*, with his *Pardon* vnder *Seale*, procured by the *Prince* to acquit him from death? Verily *all of vs* (besides the *actuall* breaches of Gods Law committed by our selues) were *non prius nati, quàm*

quàm damnati as, Saint *Bernard* saith; No sooner borne, then condemned, & vnder the Sentence of death. The *halter* was about our neckes, and we ready to bee *turned off* the Ladder; there was but a *puffe* of ayre, a small blast of *breath* in our nostrils, betwixt *vs* and *Hell-fire*, betwixt our temporary life, and endles tormenting death. The Minister comes *to vs* (at the Sacrament) with a *Pardon* from the *King of heauen*, procured by the death of the *Prince of our Saluation*, Iesus Christ, *sealed* with his precious blood: and haue not we *iuster cause*, thinke you, to *reioyce* for our deliuerance *from Hell*, then the *Malefactor* hath for his deliuerance from *Tyburne?*

3 If our Soueraigne Lord the King were iustly fallen into

to hatred and *enmity* against any of vs, and should *bend himselfe* and the *strength of all his Subiects*, to bee reuenged on *Him* for his rebellions; what a pitifull taking would that partie bee in? how glad would he be of *any* that would procure, and could assure him of the *Kings fauour*, and perfect reconciliation vnto him? And were not all of vs by *Nature Filij iræ*? and by dayly multiplication of rebellions against God, *professed enemies* to God, and God enemy to vs? Our Sauiour by his death, wrought our *peace* and *atonement*; our perfect reconciliation with God. *When we were enemies, we were reconciled to God by the death of his Son*. And, to assure our soules of this our peace and reconciliation with GOD,

Ephes.1.3.

Rom.5.10.

Christ by his Minister, *in the Sacrament of his body & blood, doth passe it vnder Seale* to euery particular worthy Communicant.

4 IF, being not borne to *any foot* of land, his *Maiestie* should bestow vpon any of you a whole *Shire* to be yours for euer; I know *that person* would thinke himselfe an *happie man*. But behold, the *King of Heauen* doth assure euery *worthy* Communicant, not of a *Shire*, but of a most *spacious, ample,* and *glorious Kingdome,* to bee possessed and enioyed, not for the *Euer* of *Time* in this life, but for the *Euer* and *Euer* of eternitie: And haue we not good cause to me merrie and ioyfull then? God is *True, and faithfull of his word and promise*: and wee know

that

that Hee by the Sacrament doth make *every true penitent Beleeuer* as sure of his eternall Kingdome, as *any Prince* (if he suruiue) can be sure to inherit his Fathers *Crowne*. For *by it*, wee are all made *Heires of God*, and *Ioynt-heyres* with Iesus Christ, who is the Heire of all the world.

Rom. 8. 17.
Heb. 12.

So that, as I said, *wee haue all* iust cause of mirth and ioy: and would to God, wee could all bee so *truely merry* and *ioyfull* as wee should bee, *both in body, and in Soule*; that *not onely* our Soules *may bee ioyfull in the Lord, and reioyce in his saluation*; but that all our *Bones may say, Lord, who is like vnto thee?* Let vs therefore, whensoeuer wee receiue this Sacrament, bee merry *a Gods Name*: Let vs *leape, reioyce*, and *exult* for our Redemption and saluation wrought by Christ : but let vs not reioyce in *surfetting and drunkennesse, nor in chambering and wantonnesse*, nor in painted *Pride and haughtinesse*. For this is not to reioyce *in the Lord*, but *against the Lord* ; this is not to bee merry *in Gods Name*, but *in the Deuils name*.

And for all these benefits whereby both our bodies and Soules may *thus iustly* bee rauished with Ioy, the Lord our God exacteth *no great matter* at our hands, but that which we may pay without any *trouble* or *dammage* to our selues; and that is (as I said before) our loue to God *for his owne sake*, loue to our neighbors, *for Gods sake*, *Math*. 22. 27. Thou shalt loue the Lord thy God, &c. And

And thy neighbour as thy selfe. Which words do include the summe of the *Morall Law* comprised in the *ten Commandements.* Which the Lord would haue vs to *obey by the grace* of his holy Spirit; & *so* to *fulfill the righteousnesse of the Law* by *new obedience,* Rom. 8. 4. *which cannot* be done, but by the *accepting* and *assisting grace of Gods Spirit*; and the *Spirit* is not ordinarily giuen, but *petentibus eum,* to *such* as *aske him* by *prayer,* Luke 11. 13 *Which Prayer,* is *Situla gratia,* the *bucket* of *grace*, whereby wee doe receiue *grace* from God to *enable* vs to fulfill his commandements.

ANd the *chiefe* of *all prayers* is *that* which our *Sauiour* taught his *Church,* Luk. 11, 2, 3, 4. when yee *pray,* say,

Our Father which art in Heauen; Hallowed bee thy Name, &c.

Which Prayer consisteth of two generall parts : { *A Preface.* / The *Petitions.*

The *Preface* is in these words, *Our Father which art in Heauen*: which containeth *two reasons*, (as it were *two props* or stayes to support *our hope* and confidence in God :) to perswade our selues that *hee will* heare our prayers and *grant* our requests. The first *of these* is his *loue* and *goodwill* towards vs;

vs; in *this word* (*Father:*) the *second* is his *power* and ability to performe what we aske in *these* words; (*which art in Heauen:*) For *earthly fathers* may haue a goodwill to helpe their children, and yet *want power* and ability to doe it; but our Father which *is in Heauen*, being the God of *all might* and *power*, hath *power to doe for vs aboue all that wee can aske or thinke*, *Ephes.* 3. 20. wee may build vpon his *Goodnesse*, and readinesse to doe vs good, because

cause he is our *Father*, for what *Father* (though euill) but desires to *giue good things to his children*? *Luk.* 11. 13. And because hee is not an *earthly father*, (who many times doth lacke power and abilitie) but *such an one* as is in *Heauen*, and hath *al power* at his command, wee need not to stagger or *doubt*, but that he *will* perform vnto *vs*, what *good thing* so euer we aske: if wee doe not *aske amisse, Jam.* 4. 3.

Now this *pronoune* (*Noster,*)

ster,) or *Our*, which stands in the *Front*, doth teach vs not to pray for our selues *alone*, but for *others* also; euen for al *our Brethren*: Desiring our heauenly Father to heare *vs* for *them*, and *them* for *vs*; and our eldest Brother and head Christ Iesus for *vs all*. Wherefore, we doe not finde, either *Meus*, or *Mihi*, or *Me*, in the *singular* Number; but *all pluralls*; as *our* Father, Forgiue *vs*, giue *vs*, leade *vs* not, &c.

The *Petitions* are by *some late*

late *Writers* numbred but *six*: but the *Fathers* & the *Schoolemen*; all the followers of Dr *Luther*; *Aretius*; and Dr *Cox*, sometime Bishop of *Ely*, (who was *one* of *those* that were at the *composing* of the *Booke of Common Prayer*,) do reckon seuen Petitions; as you may see by the *Stanza's* in D. *Cox* his *Lords Prayer* at the end of our Psalme-booke. And therefore *his* most Excellent *Maiestie* hath likewise diuided the *Petitions* into seuen.

In

In these seuen Petitions our Sauiour teacheth *what things* wee ought to desire, and in *what order* wee ought to desire them.

Petition is nothing but *expreßio & explicatio desiderii*, the *expressing* and opening or manifesting of *our desire*.

And our desire fasteneth either vpon
- *Good things*, to be obtained which is called *comprecation*.
- *Euill things*; to bee remoued from vs, which is called *deprecation*.

The *good things* which wee com-

comprecate and desire to attaine vnto *befoure*:

Whereof, { *One*, concerneth *God*. *Three*, concerne *our selues*.

1 That, which *concerneth God*, is the *hallowing* or sanctification of his blessed *Name*. *This* we are to desire and pray for in the *first place*; euen *aboue* and *before* the *saluation* of our *owne soules*. Gods glory and the honour due to his Name is to be sought for *first*, and to bee *preferred* before whatsoeuer doth concerne either our *bodies*

dies, or our *soules*. Therefore the first Petition is ; *Hallowed be thy Name.*

Of those *three good things* which concern *our selues*; The *first* is *eternall*, and hath respect *both* to *soule* and *body* ; and that is, *blessednesse*, or euerlasting happinesse and *saluation*.

The *second*, is *spirituall*, and pertaineth to the *soule* in this life ; and *that* is *Grace*.

The *third* is *temporall*, and *chiefely* respecting the *bodie* here in this *world* : and that is the

the *necessaries* fit for vs in this life.

2 That which concerneth the *eternall* welfare of Soule and body *both*, is the *first* and *greatest good* thing that pertaines to *vs* : and that is euerlasting *saluation* in Heauen, in the *kingdom* of glory. Wherefore our *second* Petition is, *Thy Kingdome come*. For we are to seeke for saluation *aboue* & *before* any other good thing which concernes *our selues*, *Math.* 6. :3. Seeke yee *first* the

the *Kingdome* of God.

3 The *next good* thing that can pertain to *vs*, is such wherby our *Soules* may be bettered; and *that* is the *Grace* of Gods Spirit; therefore in the *third Petition* we pray, *Thy Kingdome come* : wherein we desire of God, that he would giue vs his *grace*; that, by *it*, we may be *inabled* to doe his *will*, and fulfill his law : which *will* and *law* of his is (otherwise, without *grace*) *impoſsible* to be done or fulfilled by vs, by reason of

the *infirmity* of our *flesh*, *Rom.* 8.3. So that in this *Petition* we pray for the *MEANES* whereby wee may attaine to our *end* (that is, to *saluation* in the Kingdome of Glory) and that is *grace* to doe *Gods* will. The Lord God will giue *grace* and *glory*, saith the Psalmist.

This Clause (*In earth as it is in heauen*) ought to be referred to *all* and *each one* of the 3 Petitions going before: as *Gabriel Biel* hath well and rightly obserued out of S. *Chrysostome*.

stome. Biel in Can. Miss. Lect. 69.

4. The last and *least* of all *good things* which pertaine to *vs* (and yet which are by the *most* men made *most* accompt of) are *temporall goods*, such as doe concerne our *bodie chiefly*, as *meat* and *drinke*, *apparell*, *wealth*, &c. which are (by an *Hebrew* phrase) comprised vnder the name of *Bread*. And therefore in the *last place*, in our fourth Petition for *good things*, we are taught to pray, *Giue vs*

this day our daily Bread.

The *Petitions* wherein wee doe *deprecate* and desire the *remouing of euill*, are three. Whereof the *two first* doe respect *malum culpæ*, the *euill* of *sinne*. The last respecteth *malum pœnæ*, the euill of *punishment*.

The least euill of *sinne* is a *greater euill*, and hath formally in it more *malignity*, more of the *nature* of *euill*, then the *greatest* euill of *punishmet* (euen then *Hell* it selfe) can haue: because

cause *sinne* is more *directly opposite* and *contrary* to the nature of *good*, and of *God*, then *punishment* is.

Yet of *sinnes, all* are not of the like *scantling*; *some* are *more euill* then *others*. Sinnes *past* and *gone*, are *more euill* then those which are *not as yet*, but in the *future* onely.

5 Wherefore in the *fift petition* we desire of God, that he would remoue from vs the *greatest of euils*, and *those* are our sinnes *past*, and committed already

ready: which are *most directly* contrary to his goodnesse and holinesse. Therefore we pray that God would *forgiue vs our trespasses* and sinnes. And there is a *motiue* added. For euen *we* (who in respect of the boundlesse *ocean* of thy mercy, haue scarce *one drop* of mercy and compassion in vs) *are content to forgiue such as haue offended vs.*

6 In the *sixt Petition* wee pray against *sins to come*, which are in *degree* next of all to that

grea-

greatest euils; that is, to sinnes *past* and already committed: therefore we are taught to say, *Lead vs not into tentation*: that is, Lord wee beseech thee to stop the *running issue* of sinne, that it *encrease* not vpon vs, and by tempting *preuaile* ouer vs; but giue vnto vs euer the *issue* with the *tentation*.

7 In the *seuenth*, we aske for the remouing of all *euill*, which, for our sins, we might deseruedly *suffer*; that is, from all euill of *punishment*, whether

temporall here, or *eternall* hereafter. Therefore we pray, *Deliuer vs from euill.*

And *pro iis laborandum, pro quibus orandum,* saith an holy Father: wee must looke that we be not wanting to the *grace* of God, but that *we* doe earnestly *labour* for *those* things that we are to *pray* for: otherwise wee shall *mocke* God, and our *very prayer* shall bee turned into *sinne.*

But for the *edification* of the simpler sort of people, it shall not

not be amisse, I hope, to recapitulate the *summe* of this *absolute Prayer* in the compass of a short *Paraphrase*, thus:

O Eternall *Father* of our blessed Lord and Saviour *Iesus Christ*, and in *him*, the Father of *vs all*; who though thou fillest *all things* with thy presence, and art in *all places*

Our Father

places at the same instant, yet thou doest *manifest* and shew thy self most *especially* vnto vs (in *Majestie, Power*, and *Glory*) frō the highest *Heauens*: grant that *we* on *earth*, *as well* as thy *Angels* and *Saints* in *Heauen*, in all our thoughts, words and deeds, may giue *feare, reuerence, praise*, and *glory*, to thy holy and *great name*,
where-

Which art in heauen,

1 Hallowed be thy name,

wheresoeuer we find it placed by *Thee*.

Let not *Sinne* and *Satan* reigne and rule in our *harts*, but reign thou *here* by thy holy *Word* and blessed *Spirit*: That *we* being established in thy Kingdome of *Grace*, may loue, and like, and seek after the Kingdome of *glory*, with as much *zeale* and earnestness of affection here on earth

2 Thy Kingdome come,

earth, as thy glorious *Angels* and blessed *Saints* (who are rauished with the pleasures thereof *already*) do loue & affect their owne happinesse and saluation.

And for as much as wee can *neuer* attaine to *saluation* hereafter, except we *here* do fulfill thy *will*, and obey thy *lawes* : & because *no man* since the fall of *Adam*

3 Thy will be done;

Adam (our blessed Saviour *Christ* excepted) without the *speciall* assistance of thy *Grace*, can (by reason of the *infirmity* of the *flesh*) *obey* thy *will* and *fulfill* thy Lawes; therefore, gracious *Father*, grant vs the *grace* of thy blessed *Spirit*, that *we* (walking not after the flesh but *after the spirit*) may fulfill the *righteousnesse*

In earth as it is in heauen; (*Which is to bee referred to all the three petitions before rehearsed.*)

teousnesse of thy Law.

And that faithfully, sincerely, and diligently; euen as *thine* holy *Angels* and blessed *Saints* in *Heauen* doe performe it.

And because the *indigencies* of our flesh are *manifold*; in so much, that except we haue *food & rayment*, and other necessaries of life, we cannot find contentment, 1 *Tim.* 6.8

And

And so wee may bee *hindred* from walking in our seueral *callings* with that *alacritie* which we ought; nor can set our selues to do thy will so *chearfully* as we should: therefore (good Lord) let vs not lacke *these temporall things*, without the which we cannot *serue Thee*, but bestow on vs all things *necessary* for this life; whe-

4. Giue vs this day our daily bread,

whether *more* or *lesse*; and, with *them*, giue vs *contentment*; teaching our hearts to *rest* vpon thy *prouidence* in *all estates*.

5 Forgiue vs our trespasses,

Accept the *passion, death, obedience,* and *righteousnesse* of thy deare Son Iesus *Christ,* as a full discharge for *all* our *sinnes*; and in *him*, *forgiue vs*, and accept vs as *Righteous*: for euen *we* our selues, who

to the Sacrament.

who haue not the *least drop* of mercy in vs, in comparison of *thee*, are content, by thy *grace*, to *forgiue* the iniuries done vnto vs by *Friend* or *Foe*.

 Though the *Flesh*, the *World*, and the *Deuil* do many wayes *prouoke* vs to sinne; yet, in *thee*, let vs *ouercome* them and all their *tentations*.

 T Suffer

As we forgiue them that, &c.

6 *Lead vs not into temptation.*

Suffer vs not to bee tempted *aboue* our strength; but as thou sufferedst vs to bee *brought vnto* it; so, good Lord, stand *by vs*, let vs not be ouercome in it: but leade vs *back again* out of it, by the gracious conduct and *guidance* of thy blessed *Spirit*.

Gracious God, by our manifold *sinnes* wee are become subject

7 But deliuer vs from euill.

iect to manifold *euils* and *miseries*: To *eternall* miseries in Hell, to the *internall* miseries of a tormented conscience, to *externall* miseries in bodie, goods, and good name; partly by the malice of *Satan*, and partly by the malice of *men*, who are his *instruments*, and sometimes by *thine own* immediate hands. *Good Lord,*

Lord, thou *God* who hast *all things* vnder thy *power*, and *canst deliuer whom* & *when*, and *how* it pleaseth thee; O *deliuer vs* frō these *euils*; if not, by taking them *away*, yet by granting vs *patience* to endure them *quietly*, and to expect a *release* from them in *thy due time* when *thou* thinkest *fittest*.

Till *then*, most mercifull

cifull Father, grant we may *labour earnestly* for *every one* of *those* things which thou hast taught vs to *pray for*. And giue *our Amen* & assent of *Faith*, to *whatsoeuer* Petition thy blessed Son hath taught vs to make. To whom with *thee* and the *holy Ghost*, three *persons* and *one* euerliuing *God*, bee all *honour*, *worship*, *praise* and

and *glory* world without end, *Amen*.

But his *Sacred Maiesty* hauing so diuinely explicated *this prayer* of our blessed Sauiour, I shall but light a *Candle before the Sun*, if I should presume to speake any farther of it. Wherefore I will for the helpe of *some* deuout Communicants, adde a short Prayer or two to direct

rect their deuotions *before* and *after* the receiuing of the Lords Supper.

A Prayer to be said before the Receiuing of the Holy Communion.

ALmightie and euerlasting God: behold I come to the *Sacrament* of thine onely begotten Sonne; our Lord and Sauiour Iesus Christ: I come as a *sicke patient* to a life-giuing *Physician*; as an *vncleane* Lazar, to the euer-springing *fountaine* of mercy; as a blind man to the euer-shining *Sunne* of Righteousnes; as a *poore* and *needy* Begger to the Lord

T 4 and

and *right owner* of heauen and earth: as *naked* to the *Lord* of *glory*; who hath put on *glorious apparell*, and girded himselfe with *strength*. I beseech *thee* therefore (O thou *boundlesse abundance* of vnlimited bounty and mercy) to vouchsafe to *cure* my sicknes and *infirmitie*: to *wash* away my pollution and *filthinesse*; to *enlighten* my *blindnesse* and darknesse; to *enrich* my neediness and *pouertie*, and to *cloath* my loathsome *nakednesse*; that *I* may receiue the *bread* of *Angels*, the *King* of all *Kings*, and *Lord* of all *Lords*, with *such* and so great *reuerence* and *humilitie*; with *such* and so great *contrition* and *deuotion*; with *such* and so great *purity* and *faith*; with such *Resolution* and

and intention, as may be most expedient for the saluation of my *poore soule*. Grant vnto mee (O *gracious God*) I humbly beseech thee, that I may not receiue the *sacramentall* elements of *bread* and wine *onely*, but that I may receiue the *inward* and spirituall *grace* and vertue of the body and blood of Christ *also*. Grant mee, O Lord God, so to receiue the body and blood of thine onely begotten Sonne, my Lord and Sauiour Iesus Christ; that I may obtaine the *fauour* to bee *incorporate* into his Mysticall *bodie*, and to bee *numbred* amongst his *liuely members*. Most louing Father, grant that *one day* I may eternally behold thy blessed Sonne *face* to *face*, whom

I

I *now* doe onely see *darkely* in a mysterie. Grant this, for thy deare Sonnes sake, who liueth and raigneth with thee and the Holy Ghost euer one God world without end. *Amen.*

A Prayer to be said after *the* Receiuing of the Holy Communion.

O Lord, holy Father, Almightie and euerlasting God, I render vnto thy diuine Maiesty most humble & hearty *thanks*, for that thou doest vouchsafe to feed me, in this *holy mysterie* of thy heauenly banquet, with the precious *body* & *blood* of thy deare Son. *What* is there in Heauen or in Earth *more precious* and excellent then

then that *diuine body* vnited *perſonally* to thine eternall *Sonne*? What *more certaine* teſtimony, what more ſure *pledge* of thy *grace* and fauour towards *mee*, then that ineſtimable *price* of thy Sons blood, which for *my ſinnes* was powred out vpõ the Altar of the Croſſe? Thou giueſt vnto *me the very price* of my Redemption, that thereby thou maiſt aſſure my ſoule of *thy* gracious *loue* and fauour towards *me*. So often as by my tranſgreſſions I haue (*as much as in me lyeth*) caſt my ſelfe *out* of the *Couenant of Baptiſm*: ſo oft, by vnfained *Repentance* and the *right vſe* of this bleſſed Sacrament, is there an *entrance* opened for me to *returne* to the ſame *againe*. It is a Sacrament of the *New Teſtament,*

stament, and doth euer blesse & enrich my soule with *new gifts* and *graces*. In *this* body life *it selfe* doth dwel, therefore *it* doth refresh and *quicken* me to *eternall* life. By the effusion of *this* blood, there is *full* satisfaction made for *all my sinnes*: Therefore, by *drinking thereof*, the pardon and remission of *all my sinnes* is confirmed vnto mee. *Christ* saith, the *Truth* hath spoken it, Whosoeuer shall eate *my flesh*, and drinke *my blood*, hath *eternall life*, and I will raise *him* vp at the last day, *Ioh.*6. 5.4. Namely, to *glory* and *immortality*. For this is the *Bread* of *Life* which came down from Heauen; that whosoeuer eateth thereof, may not *die*, but *liue for euer*, *Ioh.* 6.5. It is the eating *by faith*,

faith, which Christ doth (in *that* place) commend; which must *necessarily* bee added to our *sacramentall eating*; that so, *that* which was ordained for life, may *by vs* be *receiued* to life. I came therefore to this heauenly banquet, in *true faith*, being assuredly perswaded that *that body* which I feed vpon *in soule*, was deliuered to death for *my* sake & for *my behoofe*: That *that blood*, which I drinke, was shed for the *discharge* and remission of *my sinnes*.

I cannot doubt, at all, of the remission and forgiuenesse of my sinnes; seeing that *that* is confirmed vnto me, by the *participation* of the *very price* which was offered and tendered for my sins. I cannot, in any wise, doubt of of *Christ his inhabiting* and dwelling in me; seeing that hee doth *seale it* vnto *me*, by communicating his bodie and blood. I cannot doubt at all, of the helpe and assistance of God the *holy Spirit*; seeing *my weakenes* is strengthened with so *sure* and strong a *fortification*. I feare not the *sleights* and *stratagems* of Satan, seeing that this *food* of *Angels* doth strengthen me to *battell*. I am not afraid of the *enticements* and *allurements* of the flesh; because *this life-giuing* and *soule-sauing* food doth comfort mee with the strength of the Spirit. *These*, being taken and digested, doe cause that Christ *dwels* in me, and I in Christ. That *good Shepheard* will not suffer a *sheepe* fed with his *owne body*

body, to bee deuoured by the *Infernall Wolfe*: nor will he permit the *strength* of the Spirit to bee conquered & vanquished by the infirmity and *weakenesse* of my flesh. O *Lord God* and *Sauiour* of my *soule*, let me *feele dayly* the vertue and *force* of thy *death* & bloodshed, to *kill* and mortifie *sinne* in my *earthly members*; that as I am made *partaker* of the *Death* of thy Sonne, so I may be partaker of his *Resurrection*, by putting on the *new man*, and walking in *newnesse of life*. Grant this for thy *Sonnes sake*, to whom with *Thee* and the *Holy Ghost*, be all praise honour and thanksgiuing now and for euermore.

Amen.

FINIS.

Gentle, Reader I entreat thee to mend these faults before thou reade the booke. others there be: but of no moment.

PAg. 46 line 10, for *Charity*, read Faith. p. 38 l. 12 r. as a fit. p. 69 l. 13, r, defensiue. L. 15, r. offensiue. p. 76 l. 6 r. of his pag. 123 l. 7 *dele* in. p. 143 l. 17, r. tastes. p. 153 l. 3, r. into. p. 167 l. 9 ϲϵϱαλαβϵῖν, r. μϵταλαβϵῖν p. 183 l. 15 *Mese*, r. *Moses* p. 185 marg. r. can 21 p. 194 l. 5, *del.* Man. p. 217 l. 6, r. then. p. 210. marg. r. Philip. 4. 14.

C 10861 X
59722

REPRODUCED FROM THE ORIGINAL
IN THE HENRY E. HUNTINGTON
LIBRARY AND ART GALLERY.
FOR REFERENCE ONLY.
PERMISSION NECESSARY FOR
REPRODUCTION.

Lightning Source UK Ltd.
Milton Keynes UK
UKOW021940240312

189541UK00005B/32/P